HIT & RUN

THE RISE—AND FALL?— OF RALPH NADER

RALPH DE TOLEDANO

$\mathbb{A}$RLINGTON HOUSE·PUBLISHERS
NEW ROCHELLE, N. Y.

Copyright © 1975 by Ralph de Toledano

Manufactured in the United States of America

Library of Congress Cataloging in Publication Data

De Toledano, Ralph, 1916–
  Hit and run: the rise—and fall?—of Ralph Nader.

  1. Nader, Ralph. I. Title.
HC110.C63D48   340'.092'4 [B]   74–26880
ISBN 0–87000–287–2

Contents

1

Savonarola in Blue Serge

ON OCTOBER 31, 1971, THE *New York Times* WAS HOST TO A full-page advertisement signed by Ralph Nader and sponsored by Public Citizen, Inc., one of the many organizations he has created. Its style was hortatory, its factual content negligible—the product of a sharp and driving mind which, however one might regard its owner, had mastered and exceeded the methodology of Madison Avenue.

"Dear Fellow Citizen," the advertisement began.

Imagine that 25 or 30 years ago citizens concerned about the future quality of life in America had gotten together to do something about it.

Suppose they had begun an effective citizen's campaign to make government agencies and industry management sensitive and responsive to the needs of the people. The *real* needs of *all* the people . . .

We would long ago have rid ourselves of the inexcusable pockets of hunger and poverty in our land of plenty. Long before the '60s we would have begun to reduce the unspeakable massive suffering of the "other America."

Our urban centers would not be choked with cars, or laced with concrete belts that strangle the polluted cities in ever-increasing slums, corruption, crime, noise and public waste.

Our rivers, lakes, and oceans would still be producing untainted fish and would be safe for swimming. The air would not be as filled with vile and violent contaminants, and the land would not be ravaged by insensitive corporate and government forces wasting our resources faster than they are replenished . . .

Thousands of American workers would not be dying or sickened each year because of toxic chemicals, gases and dust that pervade so many factories, foundries, and mines . . .

There can be an end to mass injustice if enough private citizens become *public citizens* . . .

Please mail the coupon and your check for $15 or more to help Public Citizen continue and expand the work that is already under way . . .

There was nothing particularly unusual about this advertisement, and it appeared in many publications around the country. For many years, Americans had sent in their checks and money orders for the handy exerciser which would make them the sex object of the local beach, the joyous elixir which would restore potency or expand the bust dimensions, the secret writings which would unlock the doors of universal knowledge or provide instant success. What made the Nader appeal unusual is that many thousands of otherwise sophisticated people contributed their fifteen dollars or more to the extent of well over a million unaccounted-for dollars in the belief that their contributions would end the real and/or imaginary ills of America. Ralph Nader's pitch would have delighted W. C. Fields, but those who said so were subject to instant excommunication by the multitudes of Nader's "the earth is flat" supporters.

In short, the Nader movement was one of those phenomena which from time to time seizes the American people. Whatever he said was *ex cathedra*, no matter what the facts. The Corvair was a creation of the Devil thrust upon the American people by conspirators in Detroit. After-shave lotion, soft drinks, and eye shadow were destroying the American people and robbing their purses. A handful of nuclear power plants was driving the nation into one vast cancer ward. The government from top to bottom was corrupt, and even the most zealous consumerists and environmentalists—Nader excepted—were tainted. The corporate community was bent on wiping out its customers. Pollution was everywhere. People were having too many babies and too much fun. The end of the world was upon us, and only Ralph Nader could save it. Those who doubted had only to turn to the *Washington Post* or the *New York Times* to have their faith restored.

Were Ralph Nader a conscious charlatan, he would have posed no problem. The academicians who examined his theories and found them strangely synonymous with those of Benito Mussolini's corporate state could have spoken their piece and silenced him. Objective commentators could have examined his strictures against that company or this product and demonstrated that in most cases they were based on passion and rhetoric, with little relation to fact. When he charged that United States Steel was starving education in Kentucky by paying almost no taxes, a three-line publicity release from that corporation, pointing out that it was paying 80 percent of all school taxes in the state, would have brought the pink to Nader's cheek. His Congress Project—which, according to his promise, would turn out volume upon volume of the most detailed analysis—labored and brought forth one paperback and a number of congressional profiles. But the watchdog media never called this to the public's attention.

Frighteningly, Nader—like Savonarola in fifteenth-century Italy and Cotton Mather in seventeenth-century New England—believes in his devils and witches. It did not strike him at all as weird or funny that when one interviewer questioned him about the harsh, sweatshop treatment he accorded his volunteers, he could answer, "But some of them even wanted to play *softball!*" In the City of Nader, softball, mah-jong, and television are *verboten*. Love and sex are *verboten*. In the Kingdom of Nader, there is no laughter, and only the voice of the King is heard. Those who believe that fourteen hours a day of drudgery for the King is worse than eight hours at the local legal parlor are banished to outer darkness. Nader claims that he works harder than anyone else in his various organizations—which is not true—but he is doing what comes naturally and makes an estimated quarter of a million dollars a year at it, not the five hundred he pays his Raiders for a summer's blood, sweat, and tears.

For a while, it worked.

For a while there was a very special *charisma* to the fact that he had no personal life, that he dressed in suits so bedraggled that only an oil tycoon would dare to wear them, that he lived in a grubby rooming house in Washington whose address was secret to all but half the newspapermen in Washington, that he bucked the tide and wore his hair reasonably short. To the adolescents who put their lives in his hands and the middle-aged who turned to him, a mystery figure he concocted added to his stature and his appeal. David Halberstam, a boyhood friend who had risen high in the journalistic ranks, was convinced, after talking to Nader, that he was a secret agent, an operative in the Central Intelligence Agency. And those who worshipped him most passionately and saw him as the evangelist of a new democratic affluence never stopped to think that had Nader been able, by a stroke of the pen, to deprive them of the pleasing perquisites of their daily lives— their television sets, their comfortable cars, their soft drinks and potato chips—and given them instead the Spartan rigors of more economically primitive societies, he would have done so without a qualm.

It would be unfair to say of Ralph Nader that he deliberately patterned his image on that of an astringently bad-tasting mouth-wash. ("I hate it, but I use it every day.") But as his natural temperament became known, along with his penchant for seeing conspiracies everywhere and capitalists under his bed every night, it was obvious that Nader was doing what came naturally. He did not need to take lessons from Madison Avenue. One of his biographers, almost in wonder, would write that Nader was "imperious with his staff, insensitive to frailty, and not above petty means to suit his idealistic purposes" and "blind to all that is human"—a man who "stifles dissent." Those who felt the cutting edge of his temper, and he shared it equally with the high and the low, would complain that he was "totally insensitive to his fellow man" and threw at him a line from Pogo, the Walt Kelly comic strip possum: "I care about humanity, it's people I can't stand." But this, too, was incorporated into the legend and by some perverse logic corroborated his dedication to the cause. It hardly hurt Nader at all when Senator Abraham Ribicoff called him a "fanatic"—and perhaps it helped. "This is not the time to fool around, wasting countless hours watching television or chitchatting," Nader scolded with all the intensity of a Savonarola admonishing the Florentines, "not when the future of civilization is at stake."

It took years before the public began to realize that Nader's achievements were minimal—hardly worth all the sound and fury, the damage to reputations, and the money that they entailed. The Consumer Protection Agency, to whose creation he had devoted his energies and his vituperative rhetoric, would have added a new army of bureaucrats to the overloaded Federal establishment, hogtied administrative procedures, jammed the courts, perhaps crippled the economy, and done little more for the consumer than a subscription to Consumers' Research or Consumers' Union could have bought him for a few dollars.

The six pieces of legislation for which Nader took credit in his fund-raising appeals were, by his own later averral, of no value and, in some instances as in the so-called Mine Safety Act, actually did harm. His arguments against the American automobile and his diatribes against Detroit as a conspiracy of murderers-for-profit fell apart when a reduction of speed limits to 50 miles per hour during the gas shortage saved more lives than all the seat belts and other devices demanded by Nader. Gadgetry to remove certain noxious materials from automobile exhaust had some small success, but it also spewed new and far more dangerous chemicals into the atmosphere.

In time, the law of diminishing returns began to become operative. Hundreds and hundreds of Nader hits on a bewildering array of subjects, followed by a quick run to the privileged sanctuary some of the media provided him, involved too many areas about which Nader knew too little. The victims were ignored, but there were always a few people among his supporters who knew the facts—and doubts began creeping into their assessment of their hero.

It also began to to reach the consciousness of the public. Ralph K. Winter, Jr., a Yale Law School professor who had served as law clerk to the now Supreme Court Justice Thurgood Marshall and was a Senior Fellow at the Brookings Institution, in a study of consumer advocacy pointed out that Nader was merchandising himself "the way Colonel Sanders sells fried chicken."

> It is all very well for consumer advocates to attack advertising but they themselves merchandise consumerism in a way that puts Madison Avenue to shame . . . Consider . . . how the typical "Nader Report" is merchandised. On the cover, the name Ralph Nader appears twice and in large print. The name of the actual author appears once and in small print. On the back in large red letters is emblazoned: NADER'S RAIDERS RIDE AGAIN! Nevertheless, except for the use of his name, there is little indication in these books as to what Mr. Nader had to do with their preparation.*

Nader is and was a revolutionist, but like too many of the current crop not quite certain what he wants to destroy and completely at a loss as to what he wants to build. The public has become aware of this, even as they know that he lacks a quality which the French describe in the word *serieux*. Indefatigable in attack, he nevertheless flits from project to project, never com-

---

*To defend this practice, Nader has said that he checks the texts of these publications and reports very carefully. He has, however, never taken the blame for the factual errors and interpretative snafus in these books.

pleting any particular job and seldom going beyond the flash of publicity which keeps his name current on page one or the TV news.

A serious consumerist does not accept a $3,500 fee for a lecture to his earnest adherents, allow them to spend time and money promoting his appearance, and at the last moment call to say he is "too busy" to show up or even deliver his speech over a radio-telephone hookup. Nor, having clamored for citizen participation in the implementation of auto safety regulation, does a serious consumerist chalk up a notable record of absenteeism when appointed to a Transportation Department's Motor Vehicle Safety Advisory Council, created by Congress in response to his book, *Unsafe At Any Speed*. A serious consumerist does not, within the space of two days, accuse the government and industry of wasting energy resources and also of not exploiting them fast enough.

A man deeply concerned with mine safety and the problems of the miners would not have acted as Nader did to Jock Yablonski. At ten secret meetings in 1969, Nader had urged Yablonski to run against Tony Boyle, the corrupt president of the United Mine Workers union. Yablonski had finally conceded the justice of Nader's argument that it was his duty to return the UMW to its members and agreed to run only after a promise that he would get all-out support for Nader. To this Nader agreed, did nothing, and five months before the election—when it was clear that Yablonski could not win without strong help from Nader and his organizations—withdrew, reportedly because Yablonski would not kowtow to him. ("When Nader doesn't get his own way," Ribicoff has remarked, "he strikes out at you.") Three days before Jock Yablonski was murdered by UMW goons, he complained bitterly, "I expected to get a lot more of out Ralph Nader than I ever did." Nader never went to the funeral or sent a letter of condolence to the family.

To those who gently criticized him for this callousness, Nader answered casually that he was busy—perhaps hard at work lobbying for one of his pet causes, a law prohibiting the advertising of men toiletries, products which he considers frivolous and unmanly. The media remained quiet, reflecting the attitude of John D. Morris, a *New York Times* reporter who in another context said bluntly, "I don't want to be associated with any negative stuff about Ralph Nader." A man so busy and so important in his crusade for better roach powder would never have understood the shock of Yablonski's friends—nor ever considered that for all his

14

busyness and his importance, the words of Mr. Dooley to his friend Hennessy might apply to him:

The noise ye hear is not th' first gun iv rivolution. It's on'y th' people iv th' United States batin' a carpet. What were those shots? That's th' housekeeper killin' a couple iv cockroaches with a Hotch-kiss gun. Who was that yellin'? That's our ol' friend High Finance bein' compelled to take his annual bath.

2

Nader and the Press

WINSTON CHURCHILL ONCE REFERRED TO THE SOVIET UNION AS "a riddle wrapped up in a mystery inside an enigma." Sir Winston's description could also fit Ralph Nader. This is what Nader has wanted the public to believe—and with a public relations sense that would put Madison Avenue to shame, he has manipulated the media to achieve this end. Not much arm-twisting was required, and it is only recently that a few brave voices in the press have begun debunking the Nader myth.

Yet Nader remains the hero of the "advocacy journalists," no matter how often he has been caught in gross misrepresentation of facts or in groundless and vituperative attacks on those who displease him. There is, of course, a reason for this. Nader is the living voice of all that an ideologized media believe in their hearts. He stands foursquare against American business and industry, against free enterprise, against the advertising which keeps the media in groceries. He is for government interference and government compulsion—and subscribes to the belief that he knows what's better for the American consumer than the poor slob does himself.

Far more important, Nader learned at the start the technique of newsmaking. He will throw together allegations, accusations, and a smattering of selected statistics and deliver it to his favorite reporters, who will use it, as a rule, without checking. More often than not, the story will make page one—and when those who are gored protest, their answer will appear back among what newsmen call the truss ads. "When Ralph gives me a story," one newspaperman says, "there's no point in checking it. With his spies in the government and in big business, he's done my job for me. I've got instant news."

Once upon a time, a reporter who shared that attitude would have been ushered out of the city room. But many editors share the conviction that Nader is infallible and tend to brush aside denials as special pleading by the "special interests." The skepticism which in another day was the hallmark of good journalism goes out the window where Nader is concerned, and newsmen take with no grain of salt the rhapsodic comment of Bess Myerson, Commissioner of Consumer Affairs in New York City, that "Mr. Nader is a remarkable man who, in the last six years, has done more as a private citizen for our country and its people than most public officials do in a lifetime."

Ms. Myerson's inadequacies as a public official may have been responsible for the humility of her rhetoric, however much it may have been in derogation of Thomas Jefferson, Abraham Lincoln, the giants of the Congress in almost two hundred years, and of the great reform governors like Alfred E. Smith of New York who did a little something for the people. When pressed to find substance for their adulation of Nader, the media have cited themselves or quoted *Fortune* magazine's tribute: "He is chiefly responsible for the passage of at least six major laws"—a statement which hardly takes into account the value of those laws or the work of those in the national legislature who had a little something to do with drafting them.

But Nader has put these accolades to good use. In a leaflet sent out with fund-raising appeals, he has compiled some of them modestly under the heading: "Here is what the press has said about the work of Ralph Nader and his associates." Typically, the first quotation is not from the press at all but from W. Averell Harriman who sees in the object of his affections "the courage, the knowledge, the facts, to defy one of the largest corporations in our country." But for the rest, it is the press speaking, although the passage lifted from one national magazine deletes all the critical language, in keeping with the Nader method.

"Ralph Nader is inflexible in his aims and relentless in his determination. He is determined to change America and his work is his life . . . His facts are accurate. His revelations drawn from the government's own documents or from respectable scientists are convincing. He is relevant, he is responsible, and he is usually right . . ." So said William V. Shannon of the *New York Times,* a newspaper which has some stake in Nader's future since most of his early money came from foundations which it controls.

Time magazine: "If there is a man in Washington who provokes pure awe and respect here and beyond the Potomac, it is Ralph Nader, the curious champion of the consumer. He lives his religion, devoid of greed, filled with candor, beyond influence. He has a mission. He has done it himself."

Los Angeles Times: "Nader has become, in four years, a national institution. He has brought about a near-revolution in U.S. law schools, and his influence is still skyrocketing. New public-interest groups are sprouting like daisies across the country . . ."

The Progressive: "He is not salaried, appointed, elected, or employed by any client or organization. He is bound to no predetermined issues, as demonstrated by the ever-growing assortment of topics in which he has involved himself since he began with the issue of automobile safety. Pollution, pipeline safety, radiation, the American Indian, industrial safety, law schools and law firms, food medicine, regulatory agencies, secrecy in government, and the effects of noise—these are just some of the issues associated with him."

The Times of London: "The debt of the consumer movement to Mr. Nader is incalculable. He showed the more fainthearted what is possible and proved to the consumer that he can fight back against the computerized illogic of the business world."

That Nader, without a quiver, reprints the media's catalogue of achievement, somewhat in the manner of those "testimonials" which the hated advertising profession uses to sell razor blades, raises no eyebrows. Yet somewhere along the line, his unpaid journalistic press agents should have known that Ralph Nader has said of two of the "six major laws" for which he is given (and takes) credit, that one is "a sham not worthy of consideration" and the other, a consumer-protection act, "farcical in part and deceptive in the remainder."

But the Nader coverage has not been one great paean of praise. The staid *Christian Science Monitor,* in a 1972 article by Melvin Maddocks, almost but not quite poked a finger in the Nader ribs:

> Statistics—preferably hair-raising—are used to establish the gravity and the scope of the topic at hand.
> There are 12,000 potentially toxic chemicals now used by American industries.
> The fat content in frankfurters rose from 17 percent to 33 percent in 15 years.
> Americans spend $5 billion annually on cosmetics—the pseudo-science of looking young—and only $1.5 billion on the substantive problems of the aging.
> Early on, the *Nader Report* reader is likely to feel shocked, ignorant, guilty, or all three at once. If so inclined, he may also feel paranoid, as if a secret power elite were playing him for a complete fool . . .
> The posture of a *Nader Report* . . . is all its own, and unambivalent to a fault. Nader and his raiders want action, and they use spitballs to get it. Of the regulatory agencies they have studied, the troops have had this to say:
> The Interstate Commerce Commission is a "captive" of the transportation industries.
> The Federal Trade Commission is distinguished for "alcoholism, spectacular lassitude . . . and incompetence by the most modest standards."
> The regulations of the Food and Drug Administration are a "catalogue of favors."
> Mr. Nader and his vigilantes have judged that the automobile industry has been guilty of "massive thievery," the advertising industry of "massive lying."

Increasingly, others in the media have been more pointed. *MAD,* that thoroughly irreverent and gadfly publication, in a two-page satirical spread on Nader included two items:

IDENTIFICATION

NAME _Ralph Nader_

ADDRESS _Washington, D.C._

TELEPHONE _Tapped (Usually)_

MAKE OF AUTOMOBILE _Are You Kidding?!?_

OCCUPATION _Lawyer, Consumer Crusader, Ecologist, Recaller of Cars, Destroyer of Detergents, Busy-Body, and Long-Shot Presidential Candidate_

IN CASE OF EMERGENCY, NOTIFY

Me! I'm the only one the country can trust!

RALPH NADER
"The Nation's Conscience"
Washington, District of Columbia

Dear Mr. Bobrick:

I repeat my claim that your song is "unsafe"
and should not be sung "at any speed"--as
indeed ALL songs are unsafe and should not
be sung at any speed--BY ROCK GROUPS!
Rock Groups have a tendency to perform at
extremely high decibles, this increasing the
already intolerable "noise pollution" that
is permeating our atmosphere and posing an
increasing danger to our nation's consumers.
So you see, I am not a "nut" or a "fanatic"!

Alertly yours,

Ralph Nader

Ralph Nader

P.S. I have conducted tests on the station-
ary you use, and have discovered that it is
made from trees illegally cut from the Maine
forests. Thus, you have contributed to the
destruction of our environment. Next time I
am in New York City, I will place you and
your partner under a Citizen's Arrest!

R.N.

There were others who had the courage to call Nader to task, even though, as Charles McCarry has somewhat indiscreetly admitted, those who criticized the "people's lawyer" had "their motives so enthusiastically impugned [by the media] that all the virtue they lacked became Nader's. He was perceived by reporters to be what in fact he is: the enemy of their enemies." He is also their boy, the man they have projected into the kind of power they will never have but can share vicariously.

Brock Yates, writing in *Car and Driver,* a publication which repeatedly loses advertising for its factual criticism of the automotive industry, summed up what less-independent reporters feared to commit to print but exploded in their conversation:

[Nader's] entry into the corridors of power has worked so well that [he] now reposes in a position where no one has the guts to assault him.

Why? Because any criticism whatsoever indelibly labels you as the running dog of the Big-Gov-Biz conspiracy that is out to destroy the country. With a demagogue like Nader . . . it is critical that he be surrounded by conspiracies, that every act of foolishness and incompetence be interpreted as a finely woven pattern of vicious deceit.

Therefore General Motors never simply errs by making an imperfect car, it consciously markets a lethal junker . . . The natural gas transmission companies build weak pipes for the simple pleasure of watching houses full of orphans blow up . . .

I might be willing to give him some credibility, even authority . . . if he hadn't been so grossly inaccurate in his assessment of the automobile industry . . . If he was that wrong about automobiles, how can anyone be sure his facts are any clearer about food, gas lines, pollution, etc.?

Other newsmen, more in the mainstream of journalism, have also shown a growing disillusionment with Nader and his methodology. Nick Thimmesch, a columnist who parks his shoes neither to the left or the right side of the ideological bed, has taken strong exception to the "mean, malicious Nader" whose report on *Power and Land in California* "amounts to a one-sided case against business and government figures and the California legislature as well—as though there isn't a decent person around."

This is the Nader who makes unproved charges (such as General Motors being tipped off by the Nixon Administration on the wage-price freeze) to get a headline and does not leave an apology. The Nader whose half-truths are too often ignored by advocacy journalists who pant after him like so many lap dogs for rich ladies, instead of calling the other side for their explanation . . .

His notion that employees in government and business have a duty to spy on their employers if they feel ethics are being violated, is one that could lead to some pretty sorry innings. American government and industry doesn't need a Fifth Column.

Like other newsmen, Thimmesch resented the "authoritarian" in Nader, reporting that he "phoned a girl fan of his once late in the evening to instruct her to get out of bed and go to a revolutionary film (she went, but he stayed home)."

But the press as a whole has given little currency to this aspect of the Nader character. It has a gentlemen's agreement with him not to focus any attention on his peccadilloes, not to comment on the contradictions between his much-touted asceticism and the fact that he will stay at one of New York's most expensive hotels and drive about at eighty miles an hour through city traffic in a chauffeur-driven Cadillac—if someone else is picking up the tab. Only one member of the national press, aware of Nader's screaming tirades on the right to privacy, took cognizance of the efforts by his surrogates in the investigation of Congress to uncover the presumably illicit sexual activities of members who would not cooperate.

When journalists have stood up to Nader the results have been explosive. Gay Talese, a former *New York Times* reporter and the author of several best-selling books, learned this when he attended a meeting in New York with Nader and a group of radical chic environmentalists. The discussion rang all the changes on the evils of fun city until Talese broke in with his objections.

"Mr. Nader," he said, "these aren't the problems of New York. They're signs of health. Problems are challenges and ought to be lived with. This is a city of tremendous energy. Look at the positive side. So many people don't know what to do with themselves so they've gotten into problem solving. They emphasize problems and the press is part of it. The real problem is what to do with the problem solvers after the problems are solved."

Nader was not accustomed to this kind of challenge, of *lèse majesté*. "If you don't think these are problems," he shouted, "you have no place here. In fact, I think you should leave." And he pointed imperiously to the door.

"Nader, don't you tell me to leave. And don't you tell me about New York. You're the carpetbagger here."

At that point, someone whispered in Nader's ear that his antagonist was Gay Talese. Nader's manner changed. "I'm sorry we had to meet under these circumstances," he said mildly.

But others are not so fortunate. Though Nader would be the first to argue for the "public's right to know," on at least two occasions he has threatened a nationally syndicated columnist with libel action, demanding the retraction of thoroughly documented accounts of conflict of interest within the Nader organization and the failure of the Center for the Study of Responsive Law, Nader's major satellite, to file properly with the Internal Revenue Service.* Alice Widener, another columnist, noted that Nader was a contributing editor on *Mayday*—later renamed *Hard Times*—a publication closely linked to the New Left extremists who were attempting to trash the United States in the sixties. Again, Nader threatened to sue, and when the columnist remained unimpressed, he attempted to strike at her through the editors who subscribe to her column.

It has been said by Nader critics that he is a product of the media. To an extent this is true, but not entirely. "If Nader didn't exist, the Eastern press Establishment would have created him," an irate executive said to Robert Buckhorn. But the fact is that Nader did exist. He had, certainly the widespread and uncritical support of an ideologically committed Washington press corps which always *wanted* to believe what he had to say. Without the Nader-media love feast, he would have gotten nowhere. Nevertheless, Nader has known how to milk his press support to the utmost. He is a living compendium of deadlines, local angles, and the weaknesses of members of the press corps. He also learned very early in the day that a reporter who would respond to an offer of money with a punch to the jaw can be pocketed by the leak of a sensational story.

But Nader's greatest strength has come from his ability to cash in on the friendliness of the press. If he learns that a government agency is preparing a study in a field which comes within the area of his incompetence, he will fire off a press release denouncing the agency or its head for suppressing a "secret report." The press will take this and run—and no amount of explaining will convince the reporters, who should have checked in the first place, that they are not exposing bureaucratic skulduggery. Or Nader will give a favored reporter the text of a letter he has written to a corporation president, attacking his product or his methods. Then he will mail the letter. The corporation president will be tarred and feathered, with reporters beating on his door for an answer, before he has received Nader's complaint—and by the time he has had a chance to study it, the press has moved on to other matters. If he is lucky, he will get a few inches of space in the inside pages.

The mediamen who haul water for Ralph Nader are not inter-

*Robert F. Buckhorn, a Washington "investigative" reporter and author of the laudatory *Nader, The People's Lawyer*, did not bother to investigate this case but simply repeated Nader's version and added that the writer of the column, Ralph de Toledano, had "retracted." Like other Nader apologists, he never bothered to get the facts or to ask for any explanation.

ested in any replies from corporate monsters. They know precisely what Nader is up to—and find it amusing. From any other source, they would not accept the role of press agents and partisans. As professionals, they could have long since put a stop to Nader's hit-and-run technique. But they take no umbrage, as they did not when Nader released a highly biased and prejudicial report on Chairman Paul Rand Dixon and the Federal Trade Commission. As Dixon told it to a congressional investigating committee:

> On the afternoon of January 2, 1969, I began to receive phone calls from the press and other media requesting my comments on the Nader report which obviously had been distributed to them. By letter of the same date, I was requested by the Public Broadcasting Laboratory to appear on a half-hour program . . . to reply to the statements in the reports. I informed all requesting parties that I had not received a copy of the report and was unable to comment."

A Nader staffer later told Dixon that a copy of the report "had been mailed to me that day"—that is, after the press had received its copies—and Nader blandly made a liar of his own assistant by insisting that it was all due to bad postal service. In point of fact, the report had been mailed after it was released to the press—but there is no record that any of the reporters involved took Nader to task for this calculated effort at hitting a public official below the belt. Had Dixon attempted the same kind of deliberate mischief, the outcry from the Washington press corps would have echoed in Idaho.

3

The Beginnings

FOR RALPH NADER, LIFE IS BLACK OR WHITE. THE WORLD communicates in absolute truth or outrageous falsehoods. But if one's heart is pure, then truth has a certain generous flexibility. With total sincerity, Nader believes that he is the repository of truth, both personal and statistical. To challenge him in the general or the specific is to cast aspersions on the cause to which he has dedicated himself. This makes life simple for him, but it adds difficulties to the normally complex task of reviewing his beginnings.

Take, for example, the very unimportant question of his abilities as a sandlot baseball player in his school days. To hear Ralph Nader tell it, he was great at hitting a long ball and an excellent first baseman. David Halberstam, who grew up with Nader in Winsted, Connecticut, while not gainsaying that his friend had memorized all the Big League batting averages, says of him: "Ralph was the kind of kid who, if you threw the ball at him, he couldn't catch it." To Nader, that kind of remark borders on sacrilege, not because it belittles his baseball prowess, but rather because it raises doubts about his truthfulness.

What man does not embroider the myth of a precocious childhood? But it is an article of faith in the Nader hagiography that at age four he would spend hours in the local courthouse observing the operations of juridical justice. It is unlikely that an unaccompanied child would be permitted to wander in and out of a courtroom at that tender age—and in any case, he was living in Lebanon at the time. But he insists on the truth of the legend with much of the passion that he denies the official record of his marks at Harvard Law School—a record which he insists was doctored by General Motors agents.

It may be petty to note these traits in Ralph Nader, yet they are indices of the man and of his upbringing. The son of a Lebanese immigrant who believed that continuous disputation was the door to wisdom, Nader grew up in an atmosphere which fostered the loud and critical assertion—the louder and the more critical, the more clothed in truth. It was the best of training for one who would take on the American industrial and business establishment —outtalking and outmaneuvering it and convincing the country that his truth was the only truth, no matter what the facts might be.

Nathra Nader, Ralph's father, had brought to the United States little more than a lively intelligence and a native capacity for hard work and shrewd investment. Even in the depths of the Great Depression—Ralph was born on February 27, 1934—he owned a successful restaurant in Winsted, the Highland Arms, which gave him a good livelihood and a forum for his political and socioeconomic ideas. He combined a passionate love of his adopted country with the zealous belief that he served it best by uncompromising criticism of its shortcomings—which to Nathra Nader were legion. But it is hard to believe that he dispensed with the bill of fare the kind of rancorous argument which, according to Nader biographers, gave the customers instant indigestion. He could not have been successful as the owner of a restaurant had he so belabored the people who made the cash register ring.

What seems to be closer to fact is that Nathra Nader had a bullwhip tongue which he used whenever he pleased to whomever he pleased, and that he had something to say about everything, uttering it with equal conviction whether he was right or wrong. What may have confused some of the good people of Winsted was that Arab approach which makes many Americans and Europeans believe that they are witnessing a battle to the death over principle when in reality the subject matter may be little more than the price of a pair of sandals. Beyond that the elder Nader was genuinely interested in ideas and in politics, which frequently took the form of overblown social criticism. This interest he obviously bequeathed, both genetically and by example, to his son. The difference between the two was that Nathra enthusiastically accepted the world, whereas Ralph rejected it as flighty and unmoral.

Ralph Nader's childhood and school days were not particularly extraordinary, though they may have been tinged by the misunderstandings which come of being a member of a minuscule minority among other and larger minorities of Jews and Italians in a New England ambience. Having spent a year in Lebanon with his mother and speaking a better Arabic than English, he may have felt himself set off from his classmates, but he had no difficulty with language from his first days in elementary school, and the record indicates that his understanding of English was far more sophisticated than that of his New England peers.

In high school, Nader was one of the three boys with an "A" average. He was competitive and intellectually curious—always reaching out for information, and an inveterate reader of the *Congressional Record*, a pursuit not exactly widespread among high school freshmen. If he had any social life at all, it has escaped the researchers into his past. Like Richard Nixon, he eschewed girls, dates, dances and what even then he considered time-consuming and juvenile foolishness. His reading habits were equally austere. He may have read a Zane Grey novel or two, but his tastes ran more to compilations of facts and statistics. Information was the only thing that mattered, and Plato or the ring of poetry meant nothing at all to him.

> This estrangement from art renders him, sometimes, a little deaf to the resonances of human events [his biographer Charles McCarry notes in a perceptive paragraph]. Last year in Cleveland, he was discussing the troubles in Northern Ireland. A companion remarked that it said little for the rationality of the human race that a people that was ethnically identical should tear itself apart over a religious question. Nader was amazed that the man should think the historic hatred between the Irish Catholics and Protestants was at the roots of the upheaval in Ulster. "No, no," he said. "It's a struggle for social equality, pure and simple." Joyce or Yeats would have told him differently, but there are no graphs in *Ulysses*, no statistics in *The Land of Heart's Desire*.*

In 1951, Nader graduated from the Gilbert School, a thin and unsmiling boy of whom the yearbook said, "quiet—smart—can be found either at home or at the restaurant—woman-hater." His one extracurricular activity was the dramatic club, but he never acted in its productions. He debated between Dartmouth and Prince-

*Charles McCarry, *Citizen Nader* (New York: Saturday Review-Press, 1972).

ton, and chose Princeton. There was less air pollution at Dartmouth, he said, but Princeton had a better department of Oriental languages, and at the time they were his great interest. He was probably the only undergraduate in the United States who worried about the purity of the air he breathed.

With his grades, Nader could have had a scholarship at Princeton, but his father would have none of that. He could afford to pay the bills for Ralph, as well as for the other two of his children who went to college, and Nathra Nader felt strongly that scholarships should go only to those who could not afford what college cost in those days. It did not matter to him that there were others at Princeton with families better off than his.

Princeton was a good place for Nader. It had not yet been seduced by "student activism" and the Silent Generation could even absorb a nonconformist who rejected the scuffed white bucks, the white shirt and rumpled khakis, and the blazer or tweed jacket that were the undergraduate uniform. Nader's protest was to dress conventionally—and once to appear in class in a bathrobe.

"You have a very good storage place there," Nader's mother had once told Ralph, pointing to his head. "You should fill it up." This is precisely what he did at Princeton. Though his majors were Far East languages and politics, he really went to school at the Princeton library whose open stacks policy allowed him to browse at will, picking up whatever caught his attention. He dug into old books on industrial relations or social history and ran through old issues of departed intellectual magazines. Chinese writers also attracted him but only tangentially, and he did not bother to store what he got from them in the attic of his mind.

"Nader's position at Princeton was something like that of a skindiver swimming through schools of fishes," Charles McCarry has written. He was in the school but not of it, an experience not unusual to gifted and introverted young men. He lived in the cheapest room he could find, joined the most maverick of the eating clubs, and took part in the collegiate hijinks—the water fights and the freshman-sophomore rivalries—but always as an observer. Even then he was a loner, restlessly hitching here and there. When he revisited the campus with a friend years later, his significant memories were of the academic excellence of the university and his high dudgeon when, having discovered some birds killed by a DDT spraying, he could not arouse his fellow students

29

to their peril. His closest friend seems to have been Theodore Jacobs, who later headed one of Nader's satellite organizations—Arab and Jew, comparing life styles.

The easy academic life gave him elbow room. There were no pressures, no imperatives, so he could be what one of his instructors said of him—"the best undergraduate I have known in five years." "He is not the kind of man one laughs at, no matter how different from one's own 'style' he appears to be," said another. "Ralph is a man of possible 'greatness.' " His marks slumped below average only twice as a freshman—in classics and philosophy, which is understandable—and once as a junior, in sociology. In his last two years he had a low "A" average, and he graduated with honors in the top 9 percent of his class. An academic career was open to him, and this is the path his professors wanted him to take. But the groves of academe were not for Nader. He saw his life's work in the law, and he entered Harvard's prestigious law school in 1955.

But in moving from Princeton to Cambridge, Nader suffered a sea change. The record shows that his admission test score was an undistinguished 494, though Nader now claims that this was a forgery perpetrated by General Motors to belittle him. And where at Princeton, as one of his biographers puts it, "he had been a student among the idle," at Harvard "he became an idler among the studious." Perhaps it was because he hated the traditionalism of Harvard Law School. "The icons were Holmes and Cardozo and Learned Hand," he has said. "Who the hell says a lawyer has to be like that?" He scorned Louis Brandeis and derided his contributions to child labor legislation as having come after he had made himself a few million dollars serving the Establishment.

At Princeton Nader had resented the compulsion of having to take a course in remedial English. At Harvard he was under other compulsions. The law school did not suffer his eccentricities gladly. No one considered it a sign of character when he cut classes, failed to show up altogether for courses given by professors he found dull, or disappeared for days at a time to sun himself in Florida. When threatened with failure for his cavalier attitude toward the curriculum or for not showing up at an examination, Nader capitulated to the system, in one case pleading excruciating headaches. He was also under another kind of pressure. His father's business had been wiped out by a flood in the fall of 1955, and Nader had been forced to apply for student loans which too much recalcitrancy might have lost for him.

But there were compensations. In his first year at Harvard Law, he joined the staff of the student paper, the *Record*, and before too long was its department editor. This was the beginning of his muckraking career, and it was there too that he began to develop the invective style and propagandistic brilliance that later catapulted him to fame. His first article for the paper, written in collaboration with another student, was on capital punishment, which Nader characteristically found to be "a blatant and ironically ineffective hypocrisy."

In his second year, as editorial manager, he filled almost an entire issue of the paper with an article on the American Indian —a compound of his own observations gathered during a hitchhiking trip through the West, second-hand anthropology from conversations with his sister, screaming outrage, and combative rhetorical flashes. Supporters of the Indian cause were delighted at this gift of propaganda and bought several hundred reprints to the gratification of the *Record*'s governing board. But Nader's second piece taught him a lesson. It was a factual and objective discussion of Puerto Rico's status as a commonwealth, generating little excitement. The expected sale of reprints never materialized.

When, in his third year, Nader was elected president—or editor-in-chief—of the *Record*, he proposed to use it as a vehicle for the ventilation of controversial issues and an assault on the Establishment. His fellow students—derisively referred to as "caged" animals by Nader—had no desire to see their paper converted into a propaganda organ unrelated to their lives and concerns, and Nader's fellow editors concurred. They voted him down on the nonideological question of shifting from glossy paper to newsprint —an economy device which would have given Nader money with which to buy articles from outsiders—and he quit. Three months later, he bowed his head and rejoined the staff.

It was while Nader was still at Harvard Law School that he began to develop the ideas on auto safety which would raise him to national prominence. As an inveterate hitchhiker, he had seen many grisly automobile accidents. With his propensity for focusing on an object of hate, he transmogrified his natural and understandable horror into a fury over the automobile. Two unrelated events contributed to the crystallization of his thoughts and his position.

The first was an article in the *Harvard Law Review* by Harold A. Katz which developed the theories that Nader would appropriate in his crusade against the auto manufacturers. In essence, Katz argued that if there were negligence in the design of cars—or in a particular model—the manufacturers could be held liable for any injuries sustained by drivers. Nader waved the Katz article under the noses of his friends in great excitement, though in later years he made only grudging acknowledgment of his debt.

The second event was the series of hearings held by Chairman Kenneth Roberts of the House subcommittee on traffic safety where, for the first time, the question of design as related to the incidence of accidents was raised. Again, Nader brandished the printed text of these hearings before his friends, who showed little interest. But Nader nourished the idea of manufacturer liability and used it as the topic for his third-year paper for which he got an "A"—a mark which he tartly ascribed to the inability of his professors to understand the significance of what he was saying.

In the years to come, Nader would pull together the work and the writings of crusaders for auto safety, pioneers in auto design, men like Daniel P. Moynihan who had publicized the problem, and others—bundling it up in his own "cause" and insisting on all the credit. But that was a long way off. Between his graduation from Harvard Law and the publication of *Unsafe At Any Speed*, Ralph Nader's life was a grab bag of occupations and activities, appearances and disappearances, and journeyings hither and yon, his whereabouts unknown to his friends, his addresses and phone numbers unrecorded, to the point that an experienced journalist like his friend David Halberstam was convinced that Nader was in the employ of the Central Intelligence Agency—a view that gained some credence when Nader was setting up his own intelligence service in the federal government.

For seven years, Nader lived in a never-never land, uncoordinated and grasping for the rim of a career. He talked, he argued, he expostulated against the "system" and the iniquities of the Establishment. He returned to Connecticut to practice the kind of law he had once insisted was the only duty of a lawyer, taking the small cases of harassed people that others would not take. But he grew bored.

On a spasmodic basis, he taught government at the University of Hartford. He lobbied before the legislature for consumerist bills. He knocked out a few pieces for the *Atlantic Monthly* and the *Christian Science Monitor*. He collaborated on a *Reader's Digest* article with the son of a once-famous novelist, then complained when the magazine would not publish his consumerist onslaughts. He traveled to Scandinavia and, by his account, imported the word and concept of the ombudsman, attempting to sell both to state legislatures. He visited the Soviet Union and found it bourgeois. He ranged Latin America as a free-lance correspondent for the *Monitor* and the *Atlantic*. He wrote on auto safety for the *Nation*. He was even quoted by John Gunther. When the draft board, breathing down his back, would not accept his pleas of a twisted neck and a sore foot, he enlisted in the reserves and put in six months as an Army cook. He haunted Capitol Hill as an unpaid adviser to the Ribicoff Committee looking into auto safety.

Then, in 1964, Daniel P. Moynihan, an assistant secretary of labor, gave Ralph Nader his real break, asking him to join his policy planning staff as a $50-a-day consultant. The assignment would be to prepare a report on highway safety, and Nader accepted gratefully. Up to that time, he had made no dent on the public consciousness and in Washington had been relegated to the category of the man who hangs around, who has never "had it" or "made it" and probably never will. It was from the job that Moynihan gave him that Nader really started—and from the report that he wrote for Moynihan that *Unsafe At Any Speed* grew.

Few realized it, but the countdown had begun for Ralph Nader's orbital flight.

4

Untrue by Any Standard

IT IS PART OF THE NADER MYTH THAT HE WAS MADE BY HIS BOOK *Unsafe at Any Speed.* This is true only by indirection. The book would have had a small to moderate sale, impressing those who find businesmen under their beds at night. By an irony of history, it was General Motors, the major victim of the Nader onslaught, which made him. That the publicity he received and the solicitude in which he bathed were entirely irrelevant to the book or its attack on the Corvair, the GM compact, is an additional irony.

It took a two-and-one-half year study by Senator Abraham Ribicoff's Executive Reorganization Subcommittee, millions of words of testimony, an exhaustive review of *all* the records, and a report running to three hundred and sixty-one columns of small print in the *Congressional Record* to demonstrate conclusively that Nader's charges against the Corvair and his indiscriminate smear of reputable people were fraudulent and based on a selective reading of the evidence which, consciously or not, suppressed the pertinent facts. But by this time, of course, the Corvair—a car its onetime owners still defend—had been destroyed, General Motors had been held up to scorn for "deliberately" producing an "unsafe" car, and Nader—a halo firmly cemented to his head—had moved on to matters like the aspirin content of Alka-Seltzer.

The origins of *Unsafe At Any Speed* are, like everything connected with Ralph Nader, shrouded in murky controversy. Its basic thesis, that highway fatalities are caused not by the driver at the wheel but by deliberately faulty automobile design and the inordinate greed of the auto companies, who allegedly put profits above safety and the lives of the citizenry, was peculiarly Nader's

—but it derived from the writings of others. That accident victims could charge liability to car manufacturers had come from the previously noted Harold Katz article in the *Harvard Law Review.* Daniel P. Moynihan and others had pioneered in the argument that auto design was the culprit. Nader had put it all together in inflammatory and irresponsible language, ignoring two causative factors: (1) that the major percentage of all automobile accidents are attributable to the effects of alcohol and (2) that the highest incidence of accidents can be found among drivers under twenty-five, notoriously bad insurance risks, who sit behind the wheel of a product no different than that of their elders. Nader chose to ignore the rather obvious fact that no car can be designed which can be safe in the hands of drunken or reckless drivers.

Why Nader singled out the Corvair is anybody's guess. Perhaps the sportiness of its design offended that puritanical streak in him which holds suspect anything that gives people fun. Or perhaps it was the General Motors connection which appealed to him. The Corvair was a General Motors car, and General Motors represented to Nader all that he abhors in American industry. Whatever it was, the Corvair took the brunt of Nader's attack, and in a prose given to absolutes and superlatives, he described it as "one of the greatest acts of industrial irresponsibility in the present century" —a characterization which, under other circumstances, he would have characterized as one of the greatest examples of literary irresponsibility in the present century.

In *Unsafe At Any Speed,* however, Nader was after bigger fish than one particular car. He was not merely out to prove that General Motors was producing a dangerous, almost impossible-to-handle car, or that the public was too stupid to realize it, but that automobile manufacturers and the regulatory agencies were enmeshed in a great conspiracy to destroy lives and make profits. The book was punctuated with references to "secret meetings" between government officials and industry executives, to "secret reports," and to press conferences at which officials or executives "ducked out the back door" to avoid answering reporters' questions.

This paranoid approach to a serious matter was not unusual to Nader. Long before he became known, he was complaining that his phone was tapped and warning others that theirs were too. Women who attempted to strike up conversations with him were Mata Haris out to compromise him sexually or extract from him the momentous secrets he carried in his head and never considered public property, in distinction to his attitude about the propriety of businessmen not divulging their most private affairs to him.

The tone of *Unsafe At Any Speed* was set in the first sentence of the preface: "For over half a century the automobile has brought death, injury, and the most inestimable sorrow and deprivation to millions of people." The methodology of his indictment was disclosed in one shining quotation, picked up by a few critics but ignored by the adoring media. At one point in his narrative, Nader wrote:

"Styling's precedence over engineering safety is well illustrated by this statement in a General Motors engineering journal: 'The choice of latching means and actuating means or handles, is dictated by styling requirements. Changes in body styles will continue to force redesign of door locks and handles.' " The cynicism of such a statement, if General Motors had made it, was clear and damning. But what the GM engineering journal had really said was:

"The choice of latching means and actuating means, or handles, *also* is dictated by styling requirements." (Italics added.) Nader claimed that this was a typographical error. But he could not use that excuse for having omitted the key sentence in the quotation: "Throughout the design and testing stages, the most important considerations are safety, reliability, operating ease and reasonable cost." If this was inadvertent, it certainly showed a shoddiness in Nader's research design which should have driven him out of the court of public opinion. In a court of law, the "people's lawyer" would have been rapped sharply across the knuckles for a deception of this sort.

In another instance, a drawing of the Corvair's rear suspension presumably showing how the rear swing-axle suspension results in "sudden rear-wheel tuck under" during cornering was used to bolster Nader's argument that the car was more given to overturns than any other model on the road. The diagram pictured the wheels at a 38-degree angle to the horizontal axis. But as Corvair engineers demonstrated, this is an impossibility since the car's shock absorbers prevent a tuck under of more than 12 degrees. This was pointed out by *Car and Driver* in a scathing review of *Unsafe At Any Speed*, but the drawing was not corrected in the paperback editions of the book which appeared in "revised" form many years later.*

Nader's indictment, however, was not limited to automobile design and the alleged deliberate venality of the industry. He also pointed a finger at the National Safety Council, the highly respected Automobile Crash Injury Research division of the Cornell Aeronautical Laboratory, the Society of Automotive Engineers, and even the insurance companies which have a direct financial stake in the safety of cars, as being a part of the great "conspiracy" and of deliberately hiding from the public the ruinous attributes of the American car. His obsession with corporate salaries and the inner workings of the auto industry may have made interesting reading to some, but they were hardly relevant to his thesis of consciously "negligent design." Is it any wonder that Brock Yates would have titled his critique of the book, "Ralph Nader Brings Fundamentalism to Automotive Safety (If God had meant for us to have accidents, he would have padded our heads)."

"In ways wholly unique, the Corvair can become a single-minded aggressive machine," Nader had written. "One factor has been noted in many single-car Corvair upsets. This is where the rear wheel tucks under so far that the rim touches the roadway. When this occurs, *no driver* can control the vehicle, which will be lifted up and very likely turn over." (Italics added.) Yates found this "contradictory" to tests he had made of the Corvair in 1962.

> The car was a rental Corvair with no suspension options and without any adjustment to the tire pressures . . . With three passengers in the car and running at a steady 45 mph, the driver found he could violently crank the wheel nearly a *full turn* to the right or left and, after taking his hands off the wheel, the car would seek its way back to a straight course . . . The fact remains that the Corvair stabilized *itself* in an out-of-control situation at highway

---

*Nader's answer to criticism by experts writing for automotive journals is to charge them with venality. "These magazines need the automobile company advertising, but probably more important, they require the technical assistance of company liaison men for pictorial materials and the loan of cars which they test drive and write about each month." He brushes aside these magazines as "shoestring" operations, written by "a small group of car-infatuated" people. "One can only presume that Mr. Nader spent considerably more time documenting his facts on car safety than he did in researching his assault on the industry's satellite press," *Car and Driver* responded. "It should be noted that each of the six major automotive magazines are published by by one of three substantially-sized publishing houses, two of which measure their annual gross profits in millions of dollars."

speeds without any assistance whatsoever from the driver! The particular test could not pretend to prove that the early Corvair was an engineering marvel, but it does indicate the car was far from guilty of basic treacherousness.

If there was anything deliberately conspiratorial, it could be found in Nader's careful maneuvering between design factors and production flaws—an altogether different matter. Nader attributed these production flaws to management, but had he done his homework—never a Nader characteristic—he would have discovered, as the *Washington Post* did in a notable series on the unions later published in paperback, that auto workers in Detroit openly smoked marijuana on the assembly line and soldiered on the job. In this, they were protected by the United Auto Workers, which took the position that any management interference in eradicating these practices would impinge on the "freedom" of their members and be in violation of federal labor-management statutes.

But the real giveaway and the ironic answer to Nader's insistence that automobile accidents were the result of deliberately bad design were right in *Unsafe At Any Speed*. At one point, Nader catalogued a series of "hazards" which were "born of deliberate design." They included these hypothetical situations:

—A young lady enters her garage and gets into her car to go to work. An instant later the car plummets [*sic*] in the wrong direction straight through the back end of the garage.
—A middle-aged woman is maneuvering her car out of a parked position on a busy street; suddenly the car shoots forward across the street over the sidewalk and crashes fifty feet through a store window, narrowly missing a number of pedestrians and store clerks.
—An automobile is coming out of a parking garage; abruptly it lurches forward and then careens wildly, killing or injuring pedestrians and patrons of a restaurant.
—A woman shopper is trying to back up her car from a street parking area. The automobile's front wheels are against the curb. On pressing the accelerator to ease out backwards, the vehicle does not respond; the driver presses down further on the gas. The car jumps the curb, crosses an alley to a nearby house and kills a couple sunning themselves in their own backyard.
—A couple drives into a lumber yard. The husband gets out of the car and notices that his wife has stopped three feet short of a marked area. He asks her to pull up the required distance. She shifts to what she thinks is the forward gear. (The car door is open, and

he is guiding her.) The car backs up instead; the open door knocks him down and the car runs over and kills him.

In each of these "actual" cases, the accident was caused by the failure of the driver to operate the car properly—by carelessness or inattention, or by being flustered. (It is surprising that Women's Liberation did not take Nader to task for making only women drivers the culprits.) But not for Ralph Nader. These accidents stemmed directly from Detroit's failure to take "human engineering" into account—"to identify, in advance of manufacture, the difficulties in the interaction of man and machine so as to permit the safest and most efficient operation of the vehicle by the driver." The manufacturer presumably is guilty of homicide if a man steps on his son's roller skate in a dark hallway and breaks his neck. For a fundamentalist, the act of putting a car in reverse instead of drive is the sin of the manufacturer.

Unsafe At Any Speed originated in a report written by Ralph Nader for Assistant Labor Secretary Moynihan and the Labor Department in 1964–65, "The Context, Condition, and Recommended Direction of Federal Activity in Highway Safety." During the period of its preparation, Nader locked horns with some of his superiors, who objected to his habit of going over their heads and out of the Labor Department in his attempts to prod the Justice Department to act on his theory that manufacturers were liable for prosecution because of what he saw as design shortcomings in automobiles. Just what the report stated, however, is a mystery. The report has "disappeared" from the files of the Labor Department, the Library of Congress has no copies, and Nader claims that he is in the same position—though he has supplied quotes from it to at least one writer. It is safe to assume that the contents of its 333 double-spaced pages made their way, in some form, into *Unsafe At Any Speed.*

Nader was working as a secret (and unpaid) consultant to the Ribicoff committee, then looking into the federal role in traffic safety, when he was approached by Richard Grossman, a small New York publisher, who was looking for someone to do a book on dangerous cars. Nader, Grossman's second choice, agreed to do it, and this was probably the most important decision he made in his life. No one, least of all Grossman, expected the book to be a runaway best seller, but a mix of circumstances was at work to propel both Nader and his book into the public consciousness. All of those circumstances involved General Motors.

To begin with, the January 1965 issue of *Trial,* printed by the small but militant American Trial Lawyers Association, published an article by Nader, "Patent Laws Prime Source to Secure Safer Auto Design to Reduce Highway Deaths," which struck hard at the Corvair. ATLA also began referring attorneys who had filed negligence cases against GM to Ralph Nader. He had also written a 153-page article for *American Jurisprudence Proof of Facts,* a legal reference work, in which he attacked Detroit for "building in" death/injury potential into its cars. On October 8, 1965, the *San Francisco Chronicle* previewed *Unsafe At Any Speed,* describing it as "a searing document that may become the *Silent Spring* of the automotive industry."* And on November 1, 1965, the *Nation* published a condensation of a chapter from the book under the title of "Profits vs. Engineering—the Corvair Story."

For GM, the question arose: Did Nader have a financial interest in pending litigation? This would be a very important point for the defense. In searching for an answer, however, GM's legal staff made a massive blunder by allowing the private detectives hired to carry out an investigation of Nader to probe into his private life. This, of course, was a waste of money. The detectives discovered very quickly that Nader lived a life of determined celibacy which did not admit any of the fun and games in which Washington secretaries allegedly indulge. The investigation was so clumsy that Nader got wind of it, and when two young ladies tried to pick him up—one at a drugstore near his rooming house who wanted him to join a discussion of "foreign affairs" at her apartment, the other who asked him at a supermarket to move some furniture for her —Nader became convinced that GM was trying to compromise him. He screamed loudly to all who would hear him, and on March 12, 1966, James Ridgeway blew the whistle in an article for the *Nation,* "The Dick," which compounded fact and Nader's hyper-

---

*Automotive experts and scientists, however, took a different view of Nader and the book. Dr. Robert Brenner, a pioneer in auto safety who was then with the University of California's Institute of Transportation and Traffic Engineering and later became deputy chief of the National Highway Safety Bureau, resented Nader's false accusation that the institute was funded by the auto industry. "Industry didn't give us five cents," Brenner later told biographer McCarry. "I told him that he was all wet in some of the stuff in *Unsafe At Any Speed* . . . The advocate presents his case to win it. The scientist can't do this, and that's something Ralph can't accept. There's a difference between scientific detachment and inertia, but Ralph seems to think that a careful approach to facts betrays a lack of zeal. To Ralph, there is no substitute for zeal."

thyroid suspicions. In the wave of publicity, Nader became at once the gallant defender of the hapless American driver and the victim of corporate brutality. Simultaneously, sales of *Unsafe At Any Speed* zoomed, the public somehow seeing in Nader's martyrdom the proof of his allegations.

In the hullaballoo that followed, General Motors snarled itself in a series of explanations and contradictions which served to highlight Nader's charges. When, on March 22, 1966, President James Roche of General Motors was hauled before the Ribicoff committee, he faced a packed audience in the Senate caucus room. His attempt at a denial of prior knowledge of the investigation caught him in further contradictions, and Nader emerged from the hearings a giant killer who had brought down one of the world's mightiest corporations. An invasion of privacy suit against GM also brought him some $450,000 tax-free. But Nader's real achievement was to convince the public that it was *Unsafe At Any Speed* which had been the major factor in the enactment by Congress of an auto safety law—a claim challenged by Jerome Sonofsky, chief counsel of the Ribicoff committee, and by experienced legislators who know what it takes to shepherd legislation through the tortuous briar patches of the Congress.

But the charges Nader had made, both on Capitol Hill and in his book, impressed Senator Ribicoff, who has since felt the edge of Nader's sword—and tongue. Ribicoff ordered his staff to conduct an exhaustive investigation of Nader's accusations, both sworn and via press handout and book, against the Corvair, GM officials, safety experts, and government officials in the field of automotive regulation. He was particularly interested in Nader's repeated assertions that GM had "misled" his committee, that the Corvair was known to be an unsafe car at the time it was introduced, and that the car's dangerousness was hidden from the public.

The Ribicoff committee inquest on the Corvair—following Nader's onslaught, sales had declined 93 percent and the car had been taken out of production by General Motors—was one of the most thorough and painstaking investigations ever conducted by a committee of the Congress. Every scrap of evidence, every Nader allegation, was sifted. Hundreds of witnesses were questioned and thousands of documents and technical reports were studied. For some reason, the report was never printed and issued by the Ribicoff committee. But the senator did insert it in the *Congressional Record*, where it filled three hundred and sixty-one columns. With a punctiliousness Nader did not deserve, it even included his final blasts at Ribicoff and the committee staff, charging them with bias and misconduct.

In the summary to the report,* the conclusions were categorically stated:

> For more than two and a half years, we have conducted an extensive investigation into Mr. Ralph Nader's charges that statements of certain General Motors witnesses at the hearing of March 22, 1966, misled the Subcommittee on Executive Reorganization concerning the safety of the Corvair automobile. After consideration of all the pertinent evidence, we have concluded that the subcommittee was not misled and hence there is no need for reopening the hearings for further testimony on the stability and handling of the Corvair . . . We believe the preponderance of the evidence, much of which was unavailable to Mr. Nader, is on the other side—that is, against Nader.

Citing Nader's statement before the subcommittee that the Corvair was "an inordinately dangerous vehicle" and the defense by GM officials which Nader insisted was "misleading" since it disagreed with him, the report stated that the Department of Transportation, with three independent experts, had conducted tests of the car at the Texas Transportation Institute, all of them filmed.

> After examining the data and films, the DOT concluded in July 1972 that "the handling and stability performance of the 1960–63 Corvair does not result in abnormal potential for loss of control or rollover and its handling and stability performance is at least as good as [the 1962 Falcon, 1962 Volkswagen, 1963 Renault, 1960 Valiant simultaneously tested]."
>
> After independently reviewing the test results, the panel [of experts] reached the same conclusion and added, "the 1960–63 Corvair does not have a safety defect and is not more unstable or more likely to roll over than contemporary automobiles."
>
> The conclusion of the DOT and its independent panel are consistent with the results of tests performed by Consumers Union, Ford

*Obviously, only the highlights of the report can be supplied in this account. Copies of the full report are available from Senator Ribicoff's office. It should be noted that while the media gave full and enthusiastic coverage to Nader's charges, it almost completely ignored the report's carefully documented rebuttal.

Motor Co., GM, and with statements of expert witnesses questioned during our investigation.

Nader had accused the Ribicoff committee of "ignoring" data compiled by Professor B. J. Campbell at the University of North Carolina. "We called Professor Campbell to discuss his data and its significance . . . " the report said. "Differing with Nader's interpretation of his classification system, Professor Campbell told us that it did not 'directly measure' the incidence of crashes due to handling defects. He pointed out that a car may go off the road or become involved in another type of accident for a number of reasons other than loss of control caused by a handling defect. Campbell believes that Nader has overstated the conclusions which may be drawn from his classification system." Campbell pointed out, moreover, that along with the roll over statistics, an evaluator of the car would have to take into account "its less than average number of accidents in other categories."

> We asked Professor Campbell what conclusions he has reached on the basis of his study of the Corvair . . . He told us that he had owned a '61 Corvair, driven it 70,000 miles, and was satisfied with its performance. But at the limit of control it performs differently from most other cars, he thinks. We then asked him whether he believed this difference was sufficient to justify the finding of a defect and consequent recall. He answered, "no."

Nader had charged that GM's lawyers had suppressed evidence and committed perjury in several litigations against the auto company. The report pointed out that Gary Sellers, a Nader associate, had filed a complaint with the Michigan State Bar Association on this matter. But the report quoted a Michigan judge who had heard argument on this point and rejected it flatly. Pages of highly technical evidence followed, all indicating that Nader had insufficiently or inaccurately quoted from the authorities he cited to prove the case against the Corvair. His easy charges of perjury were discussed—and uniformly rejected by the committee investigators. They also showed that GM engineers had tested and re-tested the Corvair before allowing it to be put on the market, thereby kicking a hole in a Nader contention that GM had overruled its technicians and ignored their warnings.

There was one passage which should have brought smiles to

those critical of Nader's methodology. Among those referred to with unusual respect in *Unsafe At Any Speed* was Consumers Union, which has joined hands with Nader satellite groups in a drive for automobile safety. The committee staff quoted CU's 1960 comments on the Corvair:

> The Corvair corners with very little sway . . . As to the Corvair's handling, and the sandstorm of controversy about understeering vs. oversteering and the advantages and disadvantages in relation to front vs. rear mounting of an engine, CU suggests that prospective buyers need not be unduly concerned. CU's Corvair did oversteer moderately (though less than a Volkswagen, for instance), but so to an extent do a million other cars now on U.S. roads . . .

Also cited was a CU report on tests of six compacts later that year. Corvair's handling qualities were described as "agile, accurate, feels cross winds badly," but added that "unless it is recklessly driven no unusual amount of handling skill is required; on the contrary, the Corvair in normal use controls with ease and precision and inspires confidence."

In *Unsafe At Any Speed*, Nader had quoted Denise McCluggage, a highly respected women's race and rally driver and a writer on automobiles, on the horrors of the Corvair—all of it taken out of context. The committee had written to her, asking for an evaluation of the Corvair. McCluggage had answered:

> I saw or heard no evidence of GM knowing that the Corvair was "unsafe" (at any speed) nor was there any evidence of it actually being unsafe or even difficult . . . Maybe [the GM higher-ups] were sitting in their offices rubbing their hands in anticipation of highway carnage caused by the Corvair. What I do know was that the Corvair —as I drove it—was one of the sweetest handling, most pleasant-to-drive production cars I had experienced. Most of the car-buffs felt fondly toward the Corvair from the time it first appeared. Here was what we considered the first attempt from Detroit to make a car for a driver . . .
>
> [Nader] was not aware that so much space was devoted to how to make the Corvair a better car not because the motoring journalists thought that it was a bad car but because they thought it was so much better than anything else offered to us by Detroit . . . He [quoted from an article I wrote on the Corvair] in a way which led me to suspect that he didn't know too much about cars . . . Any-

way, I have great admiration for Mr. Nader but always felt that his anthropological foray into the world of car nuts was less than accurate . . .

[The Corvair] was not really the best car, but it was better than most being offered on this side of the Atlantic at the time.

At the request of Gary Sellers of the Nader organization, the committee staff interviewed Mauri Rose, a former racing driver and test driver for Chevrolet. Sellers had insisted that Rose would be unbiased. "He told us," the report stated, "that he considered the Convair to be a stable, safe-handling vehicle. In fact, he said he tried to roll it over but could not do so."

As evidence of his faith in the car, he told us that he bought a 1961 Convair with standard transmission for his daughter. Though her left hand was paralyzed by polio when she was a child, she controlled the car well. He then told us that one night, when she was driving the car at top speed (over 80 m.p.h.), a tire blew, but she was able to bring the car to a safe stop.

Every point made by Nader in *Unsafe At Any Speed* and in testimony before the Ribicoff Committee was shown to be specious, based on inadequate information, or a distortion of fact. When the report had been completed, a copy was sent to him for his comments and for any suggestions as to its accuracy. A copy was also sent with a similar request to General Motors. His answer was typical—an *ad hominem* attack on the motives and ethics of the committee staff, neatly wrapped in a number of false allegations. He charged among other things that GM had received "highly preferential" treatment, whereas in fact Gary Sellers had averred that he had fifty hours of conversations with the committee staff presenting the Nader position. He charged that GM had been given access to testimony by non-GM witnesses, which was not true. He further charged that a staff member had shown no interest in Nader's comments on the Department of Transportation's reply to a Nader critique of the DOT report previously quoted in this account. The record showed, however, that the committee had repeatedly requested from Nader his views on the DOT response, and pleaded with Nader assistants to submit a reply. "They consistently refused to do so," the staff reported in an undenied letter to Senator Ribicoff. "We have always stated that we wanted to consider Nader's views on the DOT report and every other issue."

Had Nader complied, he would have submitted himself to the process of probative examination, which was the last thing he wanted. It was far better to make unjust accusations, as he had against the Corvair, General Motors, and its officials. As a one-man wrecking crew, he had put a fine car out of commission, cost GM many hundreds of thousand of ligative dollars, and destroyed reputations—while making himself a worldwide reputation for integrity and an undisclosed amount of money. Is it any wonder then that Murray Kempton, a brilliant writer and a leader of the New Left, should have likened Nader to the greatest devil in his pantheon, Joseph R. McCarthy?

5

The War on the Automobile

HAVING SINGLE-HANDEDLY DESTROYED WHAT EXPERTS AND ORdinary drivers had considered one of the safest and most satisfying cars on the road, the man who saw the automobile as a "psychosexual" symbol, a "stylistic demon," and a "pornographic" excrescence, looked for fresh fields of battle. With commendable evenhandedness, Ralph Nader turned his attention away from an American car and focused on the German Volkswagen, making use of "facts" and statistics with the same cavalier disregard for accuracy. As in the case of the Corvair, Nader's charge that the Volkswagen was "the most hazardous car currently in use in significant numbers in the United States" and "more likely than most other cars to cause serious or fatal injury in collision" was coupled to the far more serious accusation that this condition was deliberately built in, for reasons unspecified. Nader arrogantly demanded that production of the Volkswagen Beetle be "phased out as soon as possible" and that production of the microbus cease immediately.

The Nader blast—a 200-page pamphlet prepared by the Center for Auto Safety, an organization he had created, and bearing the names of Lowell Dodge, Ralf D. Hotchkiss, Carl Nash, Stephen Oesch, and Bernard O'Meara—bore more than the Nader imprimatur. Questioned about its contents, Nader said that he was "absolutely satisfied" with the statistics and their interpretation. "I did a great deal of work on this report myself," he said. "I didn't just supervise it."

Unfortunately for Nader, *Road & Track*, the oldest and most respected of automotive publications, also did a great deal of work

47

on the Nader VW report. It ascertained first that the center had done no independent testing of the car but had relied on materials prepared by others. *Road & Track* then compiled the entire research file used by the center and compared it to the report. When the magazine made its own report on the Nader report, it dutifully noted the accusation that Volkswagen had "spent a fortune . . . to cover up or repress the engineering truth about its vehicles" and of having used pressure to "oppose and defeat proposed government safety"—as well as having, as *Road & Track* summarized it, "distorted the truth about test results on the Beetle, thus knowingly jeopardizing the public's interests."

Solemnly, it quoted Nader's foreword to the center's report in which he mourned the "profound human devastation" caused by the VW and rhetorically asked, "Against the excessive toll of life, limb and property, can any executive of the company look deep into his conscience and say that whatever was gained was worth that much to [Volkswagen]?" As *Road & Track's* John Tomerlin examined the evidence, the question of conscience and ethics loomed large, but the finger pointed not at the Volkswagen and its makers but at Ralph Nader and the Center for Auto Safety.

Was the Volkswagen, as Nader insisted in excited prose, "the annual version of the 17-year locust"? Did the car have "collapse characteristics in a crash reminiscent of a Japanese lantern"? Did the putative faults of the VW prove the "tragic devolution of corporate character"? *Road & Track*, after evaluating the evidence, found the Nader report to be "inaccurate . . . misleading . . . misrepresentative . . . inexcusable . . . irresponsible . . . and unjustified . . ." *The Volkswagen: An Assessment of Distinctive Hazards*, it was discovered, ranged far and wide, even to an attempted proof that it was not really an economy car.

This last was achieved by citing a study prepared for the Insurance Institute for Highway Safety to show that four replacement body parts for the VW cost more *per pound* than those for the Chevrolet Impala and other American and foreign cars. What the Nader report failed to note was the small fact, from the same study, that for the Volkswagen these parts cost $145.65, whereas for the Impala the cost was $392.40—and that the VW was at the bottom of the expense list of the twenty-four cars noted by the Insurance Institute.

This is minor, almost ridiculous, but typical of the Nader report methodology. To begin with, the comparisons made by Nader were statistically unsound. The vw was the only car of its size considered by his eager researchers. "There were too few other small cars on the road at the time the report was being prepared to make comparison," the Center for Auto Safety explained lamely. In short, there were no valid comparisons.

One of the major sources for the Nader indictment was a study of the vw made by the Cornell Aeronautical Laboratory, the leading crash-injury research organization. Carefully "edited" tables from this study appeared frequently in the Nader report. On the basis of what purportedly had been adduced by the Cornell Laboratory, Nader charged that one of the vw's hazards was the seat track damage which occured during front-end collisions, giving the impression that vw seats failed more often and caused greater injury than those other cars. On this, the Cornell Laboratory stated:

> Generally, the Volkswagen seat slipped on the track less often, and tore free more often, than the seat of an American car. Differences were not statistically significant. The frequency with which tracks bent or tore free of the floor appear to be lower for Volkswagen than for American cars.

This was suppressed in the Nader report.

D. M. Severy was cited eleven times in the Nader report's chapter on seats. In a letter to Volkswagen, following publication of the Nader report, Severy wrote, "In [UCLA] tests and in more recent tests, we have found that the Volkswagen can withstand in most cases collision force of greater magnitude without failure than the seats tested for domestic and foreign cars of the same vintage." Then, with pointed clarity: "Mr. Kenneth Simons wrote to us making a substantially similar request [on the performance of vw seats] and we wrote to him in substance what we are writing you."

Kenneth Simons was a project contributor for the Nader report, and is so listed in the book. *What a respected expert had stated was suppressed.*

To bolster the argument that the Volkswagen was an extraordinarily dangerous car, the Nader report stated that the "major cause of actual injury to occupants of the Beetle is the windshield. It causes 20.5 percent of all occupant injuries. The highest for any car in the study [made by Cornell]." *Road & Track* published the table, not in the Nader report, from which this statistic was elicited. Then the magazine commented:

The first column on the left justifies Ralph Nader's claim that 20.5 percent of those injured in the Volkswagen hit the windshield. Observe, though, that if you are thrown forward in a car you must hit the steering wheel, the dashboard or the windshield. Add the total of the three columns for each car, and you will find that Volkswagen is *lower than almost any other type car.* (Italics in the original.)

The Nader report warned of the dangers of steering column penetration in Volkswagen accidents, again purportedly leaning on Cornell findings. Yet the laboratory had this to say on the subject: "Although steering column penetration was somewhat more frequent for Volkswagen than for some other cars, the proportion of steering-assembly-caused injuries that were serious or fatal was lower for Volkswagen than for occupants of most other cars." In fact, where steering assembly injury as a major cause is, for the Volkswagen, 8.7 percent, it ranges between 13 percent and 15 percent for other cars.

This, too, was suppressed by the Nader report. Suppressed, as well, was the statement in the Cornell study: "The distribution of accident severity is essentially the same for Volkswagen as for most other cars. Overall, the structural integrity of the Volkswagen compartment area appears to be maintained as well as that in any other car."

The most harrowing portion of the Nader report concerned the Volkswagen's susceptibility to burning because of alleged shortcomings in its fuel system, accompanied by photographs of victims designed to chill and horrify. The statement by Nader on the hazards of the Volkswagen was, as usual, dramatic:

> The performance of the Beetle's gasoline storage system in front-end crashes is a serious threat to vehicle occupants . . . The Beetle gas tank is particularly vulnerable because the body of the tank is above the chassis of the vehicle . . . a further hazard is the four-point attachment of the fuel tank . . ."

Nowhere were these allegations sustained by scientific or statistical evidence—in fact, just the opposite. All tests showed that in front-end collisions at varying speeds, the Volkswagen fuel tank did not split or suffer rupture. Of the many surveys on fire involvement in different cars, Nader chose one made in Sweden by someone associated with a college department of plastic surgery and based on newspaper reports of 94 accidents. This highly unscientific study asserted that front-tank cars, of which the Beetle is one, were responsible for 80 percent of the burns and 88 percent of the fatal burns in the newspaper stories.

Ignored by the Nader report was the finding of the Danish State Motor Vehicle Administration, based on all fire accidents in Denmark over a four-year period, which categorically concluded that the "investigation has not given evidence to support the assumption that cars with the fuel tank at the front are on the whole more dangerous than cars with the fuel tank at the rear as to the fire risk during or after a traffic accident." Nader's "researchers," moreover, had not seen fit to quote one of their major sources, the Cornell Laboratory, which had stated categorically that the "frequency of occurrence of fire among Volkswagens was among the lowest observed in the data."

A survey by the New Jersey Highway Authority was repeatedly cited by the Nader report. But nowhere were the innocent victims of Ralph Nader's passions informed that this report stated that small cars had a lower accident rate than standard-size cars; that the vw had slightly fewer accidents than its part of the sample; and that though the vw had a greater tendency to roll over it was better than other compacts in driver deaths, single vehicle accidents, and run-off-the-roadway accidents.

Summing up, *Road & Track* laid it on the line:

> In his foreword to *The Volkswagen: An Assessment of Distinctive Hazards*, Ralph Nader speaks of an "ethical imperative" on the part of Volkswagen to withdraw its cars for modifications. We believe we see a different imperative. In light of the total failure of the Nader Report to prove its charges . . . considering the enormous publicity the Report has received . . . *Road & Track* recommends that Ralph Nader observe the "ethical imperative" to recall the VW Report and publicly retract its inaccuracies.

Of such would be the Kingdom of Heaven. But Ralph Nader made no retractions. Instead, he loudly accused his critics of being in the thrall—or worse—of the automotive industry, shouting "Stop, thief!" at his pursuers and throwing the posse off the track. His persecution complex working overtime, he could brush aside an editorial such as the one in the *Toledo Blade* of May 1971, headed "Noise in Naderland":

Mr. Nader was testifying before the Senate Commerce Committee on a bill aimed at making motor cars less susceptible to damage and repairs less expensive. He scattered his critical shots in all directions, as usual [attacking] the auto industry for nothing less than "massive thievery" and "criminal fraud" in the way it designs its products. In response, not fewer than three senators took issue with Mr. Nader's remarks—expressing resentment of his contemptuous verbiage, suggesting he would do better to stick more with facts and less with colorful language, and challenging him to go before a grand jury if he had evidence to support a charge of criminality against the automakers.

One of the bases Mr. Nader touched some time back was noise pollution—the need to reduce the cacophony that besets us these days. We were heartily with him on that, and we still are. How greatly he might benefit himself and all the rest of us if he would start by turning himself down.

The Nader noise, however, was not limited to auto safety. He was out to punish the American car and everyone in and out of government for every facet of the automobile, its production, and its use. On April 14, 1971, there had been a widely disseminated release attacking the Department of Transportation because General Motors had added a "raised hood ornament" to its Chevrolet Monte Carlo, about which the DOT had done nothing. According to Nader, the more than 10,000 pedestrians killed every year were for the most part victims of the "sharp, slashing points and edges" of automobile exteriors.

Two days later, Nader was at it again, firing off a letter to Chairman Miles Kirkpatrick of the Federal Trade Commission in which he waved an article by a student in the *Yale Law Journal* arguing that the annual model changes in American cars—to simpler minds the result of the great competition in the industry—were made to prevent new manufacturers from entering the field and therefore an "unfair" trade practice. The major thrust of this communication, however, was a demand that the FTC break up GM, Ford, and Chrysler into smaller companies. That Detroit had been moving away from the model changes which so aroused Nader hardly concerned the "people's lawyer."

On May 10, 1971, Nader made the appearance referred to by the *Toledo Blade*, in which he accused the automotive industry of "collusion" and of a "continuing quest for greater fraud at higher prices for millions of Americans"—and of "knowing, calculated criminal fraud." Then he turned on the Senate, accusing those

52

who wrote the bill under consideration of "political timidity" in the face of the "brazenness of corporate crime" and the committee itself of "groveling" to Big Business. The sharp exchange made headlines and the television news comment programs. But Nader's failure to produce anything more than vitriol for the Senate Commerce Committee or, as the most litigious individual in the United States, to take his "case" to the courts—his duty as a citizen with knowledge of a felony—left a bad taste on Capitol Hill. To some senators it smacked of conscious manipulation of public opinion and bad faith—a suspicion later reinforced by Nader's actions in similar situations.

On July 3, 1971, Nader launched an attack on the thirteen-million member American Automobile Association, announcing in advance what an investigation of the organization to be launched that summer would "find." The AAA, said Nader, supported the "auto industry's disdain" for consumer issues like safety and pollution. Nader's Raiders, he wrote, would look into the "small but growing nationwide dissatisfaction of AAA members with practices and policies of an organization that claims to speak on their behalf." At the time, Nader "interns" had already begun what was later described as an "adversary proceeding" of considerable aggressiveness.

Instead of folding, as others had done when Nader took up the cudgels, the AAA counterattacked by asking some pointed questions, never answered: "The Ralph Nader-backed Center for Auto Safety . . . lacks the legitimate qualifications to speak either as a representative of the automobile consumer or as an expert on matters relating to auto safety . . . Mr. Nader has defined for himself the role of a consumer advocate. Is this the basis on which the Center makes it claims? Who does the Center really speak for? Is it the consumer and, if so, how do they participate in the decisions of the Center? . . . Where do the funds for the Center come from? . . . Specifically, how many consumers does the Center have and where did it obtain its mandate to speak on behalf of the consumer?" The AAA objected strenuously to Nader's "venomous tone," his "unsubstantiated attacks" on an organization he was presumably looking into with objectivity, and the "harassing tactics of your people which have culminated in their use of foul language on the telephone."

The AAA, moreover, demanded that if Center probers were to continue to be allowed to burrow in its files and cross-examine its officials, Nader would have to submit to an interview with the editors of AAA's publications to explain his purposes. To Nader, this was "one more evidence of bad faith, along with your invectives in your public commentary that have utterly no redeeming value or an iota of fact or insight"—words far more applicable to the man who uttered them. Regally, he set a deadline for a reversal of the AAA's position and a resumption of his fishing expedition. To this, James B. Creal, the AAA executive vice-president, responded that Nader wanted "one-way communication—your way." He made it clear that the AAA would not be converted into a militant consumerist organization as Nader demanded.*

On September 6, 1971, the Center for Auto Safety jumped the gun on its own uncompleted "investigation" of the Volvo, charging that the Swedish car was susceptible to premature brake wear, difficult engine starts, and poor gasoline mileage, adding the "sincere belief" that "expectations created by Volvo's national advertising campaign are monumentally misleading and deceptive." This was answered three days later by Pehr G. Gyllenhammar, president of Volvo. "Nader's report is based on replies to an advertisement which asked Volvo owners who had complaints to contact him," Gyllenhammar said. "He based his report on 140 cars, but we sold more than 50,000 vehicles in the United States this year alone. This is strange statistics."

On February 23, 1972, Nader struck out in his suit to compel auto makers to install air bags in all 1974 model cars. He had charged, as usual, that a conspiracy existed in the White House to prevent such installation, under pressure from Detroit. Then as now, the air bags were highly controversial and their effectiveness challenged, but Nader believed in them. A federal judge in Washington, who examined all secret memoranda between the White House and the Department of Transportation, found nothing to support the Nader contention that a conspiracy existed or that there had been any pressure. To this writing, Nader still clamors for mandatory seat bags—immediately—though there are no conclusive tests to show their worthiness and a possibility that they may be hazardous.

*Said John D. Morris, a Nader adulator, in a *New York Times* story: "From the outset, Mr. Nader and [Ron] Landsman [a twenty-three-year-old University of Michigan law student] have made no secret of their intention to shake up the staid auto club in the hope of bringing about its transformation into an activist champion of consumer cases. So far, they have succeeded in shaking the dignity, if not the reputation for service to the motoring public, of the 69-year-old organization." Morris did not discuss the sources of authority for Nader's invasion.

In April 1972, Nader demonstrated the methodology of his consumer advocacy by accusing the National Highway Transportation Safety Administration of dragging its feet in the investigation of engine fires. Specifically, Nader charged that the 1972 Chevrolet Vega was prone to catch fire because of faulty carburetor assembly. Reporters who called General Motors were told that 130,000 Vegas would be recalled, the implication in a newspaper reader's mind being that this action had been the result of Nader's watchfulness. In fact, Nader had learned of the imminent recall from an informant at General Motors. Quick footwork had given him the opportunity to make his charge before GM made its announcement. The media cooperated in placing the halo on Nader's head.

But in his war on the automobile, that "stylistic demon," what had Ralph Nader achieved? A story in the September 2, 1971, *Wall Street Journal* had reported:

> Ralph Nader, the consumer advocate and auto-safety critic, catalogued a long list of defects that he said existed in recent-model cars . . . Mr. Nader also charged in a letter to Douglas W. Toms, head of the National Highway Traffic Safety Administration, that the agency is guilty of "negligent inaction" in its investigation of such alleged vehicle-safety defects . . .
>
> Mr. Nader called his letter "only the introduction" to his study of safety defects and vowed he will continue to send correspondence directly to Mr. Toms "and to the public." *It's understood* [italics added] that Mr. Nader and his associates have accounts of other car-safety problems about ready for this kind of attention, having decided to to stop going through the Defects Investigation Office but to deal with Mr. Toms himself.

Is the car the cause of accidents, or is it the driver? Nader had pointedly ignored an accident study by the Cornell Aeronautical Laboratory which showed that the average driver used only 25 percent of the maneuverability built into today's automobiles. He also had no comment about statistics cited by Franklin M. Kreml, president of the Motor Vehicle Manufacturers Association, which clearly indicated that the driver was more responsible for accidents than the machine itself—something anyone who has traveled the nation's streets and highways could confirm.

> One of the major concerns of our societal leaders is highway safety, where the motor vehicle industry moved to the forefront in 1936.

Indeed by establishing the Automotive Safety Foundation that year, the industry essentially founded the U.S. traffic safety movement . . .

The resultant national program, focusing on all three elements in traffic safety—the driver, the highway, and the vehicle—in the twenty-five years following 1936, succeeded in reducing the traffic accident fatality rate from 15.1 per hundred million vehicle miles traveled to about 5. The number of actual fatalities remained at 38,000, even though, during those 25 years, the number of vehicles increased by 267 percent and the number of highway miles traveled by 193 percent . . .

There are now 44 Federal safety standards that apply to one or more classification of motors vehicles . . . A general estimate is that buyers of new model cars will, together, pay a $3.3 billion safety premium annually. Have the benefits justified this expense?

The death rate has declined about one point but the number of fatalities keeps going up, reaching a record high of 57,000 last year. And research conducted over the years in which the major safety features have been standard on all new cars indicates that, with the exception of the devices designed by the manufacturers before the 1966 [auto safety] Act, none has made a *significant* difference.

All of the wild charges, the destruction of reputations, and the denigration of American and foreign cars—with their concomitant burden of worry and uncertainty to drivers—which brought Ralph Nader fame, power, and fortune, did almost nothing for the consumer over whom the "people's lawyer" so publicly weeps.

The seriousness of the work done by Ralph Nader and his Center for Auto Safety may have been summed up in a release they issued on July 16, 1971:

Two attorneys associated with Ralph Nader today leveled sharp criticism at the Chrysler Corporation for selling to a California consumer as a "demonstrator in new car condition" the 1968 Chrysler Imperial convertible used by Warner Brothers in the film BIG BOUNCE which stars Ryan O'Neal.

There is no record that this "sharp criticism" stopped the planets in their courses or saved a single life on an American highway.

6

The Children's Crusade

"NADER'S RAIDERS" THE *Washington Post* CALLED THEM, and the label stuck. It had the felicity of rhyming cant and a large degree of poetic truth. Like all shock troops, they considered themselves an elite—the sons of the rich, for the most part, who saw themselves heroically redressing the crimes of their parents, *tireurs épatants* in the battle to save America from itself, with but a dozen women in their ranks and few, if any, blacks. The "mini-Naders," as they were also called, were cut from the same ideological cloth as Ralph Nader. They were motivated by the same implacable hatred of American industry, the same intolerance, the same conviction that ends justify means, the same airy belief expressed by Nader that "if a job is worth doing, it's worth doing badly." They were also suspicious, cantankerous, and full of the sense that they were, if not God's anointed, at least minor-league saviors.

Like much of what Nader has wrought, they came into being almost by accident. In 1968, more and more young people—particularly those with Ivy League backgrounds—discovered that they were rebels without a cause. Disillusioned by a civil rights movement which had less and less use for "whitey," they could either picket the corner supermarket for Cesar Chavez and his minuscule United Farmworkers of America or take their place in commerce and law which their parents' position guaranteed them. The rise of Ralph Nader as a St. George among the business dragons solved their problems and they clamored for a part in what was then a one-man movement.

The first seven Raiders, chosen by Nader to carry out his invasion of the Federal Trade Commission, needed no public-relations laundering. All were Ivy League and all had social credentials. Robert Fellmeth had been a Goldwater supporter in 1964. William Howard Taft IV was a great-grandson of a president and chief justice of the United States. Edward Cox, of a rich and influential family, was keeping company with Tricia Nixon. John Schultz was a graduate of Princeton and the Yale Law School. And so it went. Why they were selected remains locked in Nader's head. Taft IV outlined the process. "If you wrote him, he'd ignore you. If you wrote twice, he'd call you at one o'clock in the morning." There was never anything more than those letters and that phone call. Relying entirely on intuition, Nader said yes or no, choosing those who were to be entrusted with advocacy of the "people's" cause as casually as he dealt with facts. The major qualifications seemed to be blind loyalty to Nader and the willingness to work around the clock at sweatshop wages.

The attitude of the Raiders, later summed up by one of them, was "it's law, it's journalism, it's street fighting, it's politics." Their aim in "investigating" the FTC and other regulatory agencies was not to report accurately but to draw up an indictment, and their major weapon was to impute base motives where others more experienced would have seen bureaucratic sloth and little else. When they discovered an FTC official asleep in his office, a newspaper over his face, they saw it as a sign of deliberate sabotage, of widespread "alcoholism"—of anything but a human lapse.

The first group of Raiders descended on the FTC like avenging angels. They demanded to see confidential files, to interview everyone and anyone, to halt the operations of the agency so that they could get their evidence. When they were refused anything, they threatened to file suit under the Freedom of Information Act. Their hostility was so patent that Paul Rand Dixon, then chairman of the commission, broke off an interview with John Schultz, led him to the door by the arm, and called a halt to further cooperation. The Raiders thereupon talked secretly to officials with a grievance, of which there are some in every Washington office, and based their critique on unchecked allegations. When the report on the FTC was written, it dealt in typical Nader hyperbole:

Like an aged courtesan ravaged by the pox, the FTC paints heavily the face it presents to the public. Because the failures go deep the paint has to be laid on thick—thick as a mask. Keeping the mask painted is perhaps the one activity the Commission dedicates itself to with energy. Its working materials are public relations, secrecy, and collusion.

This comparison of a government agency to a syphilitic whore may have satisfied the Savonarola in Nader, but it was an injustice to an agency which over the years had accomplished much and which had attempted to be an even-handed intermediary between consumer and industry. But it had its effect. Under the Nixon administration, the FTC changed its role, to one of partisan advocacy of a "consumerist" activism and of antagonism to the business sector—something Congress never had in mind when it created the agency. But this did not satisfy Nader and his Raiders, who wanted the FTC to have the power to impose criminal sanctions without a Constitutionally guaranteed due process against all those who incurred its displeasure.*

The FTC report, which caused considerable furor, had one by-product. Nader assigned one of the Raiders, Christian S. White, to file a petition with the FTC to ban phosphates from detergents. With sublime ignorance, White contended that phosphates were a water pollutant which poisoned fish. Now the simple fact was that phosphates are not poisons—on the contrary, they are a harmless fertilizer, present in nature in very large quantities. They do stimulate the growth of algae—that aquatic vegetation which gave Green Bay, Wisconsin, its name long before Procter & Gamble came on the scene. When algae rot, they consume oxygen in water which *can* kill fish, by a process of eutrophication. However, as two scientists of the Woods Hole Oceanographic Institute reported, with wide backing from their colleagues, "If all phosphates from detergents could be eliminated . . . no reduction of algae or eutrophication could be expected."

This, of course, was only a small part of the point. Pressed by the phosphate scare generated by Nader and his "environmentalist" allies, detergent manufacturers began removing this necessary and harmless ingredient, replacing it with other substances of a lethal nature—to wide applause from those sharing the Raider mentality. At this point and in order to save the country from its

---

*The prevailing attitude of the Raiders toward the FTC was summed up by Robert Fellmeth, "God damn those bastards!" This was reflected in press reports which found little news in Chairman Dixon's rebuttal report, which plaintively argued: "How any group could profess to have made an empirical study of the FTC and make no mention of at least a single accomplishment is beyond me."

saviors, the Surgeon General of the United States was compelled to step in with a warning that the available substitutes for phosphates "are clearly toxic or caustic and pose serious accident hazards, especially to children . . . Such materials measured in quantities as little as a fraction of a teaspoon may cause severe damage to the skin, eyes, mouth, throat, larynx, esophagus, or stomach on contact." They were so dangerous, he added, that those using them would run "a serious risk of irreversible loss of sight, loss of voice, ulcerations and blockage of the esophagus, severe skin burns and even death." The heads of four government agencies stopped the nonsense by urging a return to phosphates in the interests of the nation's health and safety.

Nothing daunted, the Raiders pushed on. With the proliferation of Nader "front" organizations (see chart), the number of Raiders —students drawing five hundred dollars for a summer's work, if that—grew to a hundred and more. And where once they came unbidden to work for Nader, a hard-sell campaign was devised to bring them in. Donald Ross, one of the professionals in the Nader apparatus, summed up the technique at a conference of Public Interest Research Group leaders in terms that would have gladdened the heart of a Madison Avenue account executive:

> You got to think of lures. You get a catchy name—like Semester-in-the-Capital. You don't allow anybody to see the capital before the semester begins . . . Let me say something ruthless about students who are summer interns. Don't pay them more than two-thirds until the project is completed. That's a sad experience we had in Washington—the irresistible lure of a 21-day trip to Europe before school opens sometimes comes ahead of, say, finishing the report on the Interstate Commerce Commission. It's just like any other business. You don't pay until they do their stuff.

As Nader's activities expanded, new offices were opened, several of them in the National Press Building.* With cloak-and-dagger humorlessness, they bore no name on their doors although at least one of them was decorated with the Vietnam war "peace" symbol and the thunderbird red-and-black banner of Cesar Chavez's United Farmworkers Union. Young girls scurried in and out

*During this period, Nader made full use of the facilities of the National Press Club though, as a nonmember, he was not entitled to do so. When an officer of the club suggested that Nader join, he replied, "Why should I? What can the club do for me?"

Nader Network Funding-1972

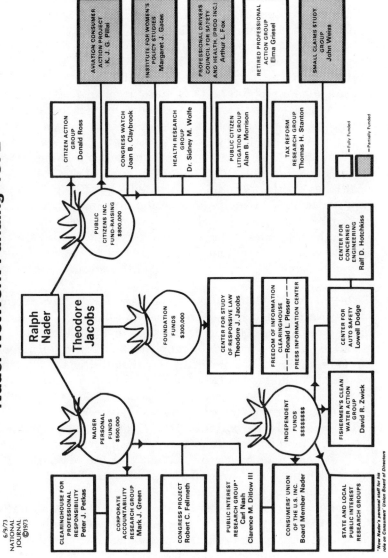

6/9/73
NATIONAL
JOURNAL
©1973

= Fully Funded

= Partially Funded

Ralph Nader

Theodore Jacobs

PUBLIC CITIZENS INC. FUND-RAISING $800,000

FOUNDATION FUNDS $300,000

NADER PERSONAL FUNDS $500,000

INDEPENDENT FUNDS $$$$$$$$

CITIZEN ACTION GROUP
Donald Ross

CONGRESS WATCH
Joan B. Claybrook

HEALTH RESEARCH GROUP
Dr. Sidney M. Wolfe

PUBLIC CITIZEN LITIGATION GROUP
Alan B. Morrison

TAX REFORM RESEARCH GROUP
Thomas H. Stanton

AVIATION CONSUMER ACTION PROJECT
K. J. G. Pillai

INSTITUTE FOR WOMEN'S POLICY STUDIES
Margaret J. Gates

PROFESSIONAL DRIVERS COUNCIL FOR SAFETY AND HEALTH. (PROD INC.)
Arthur L. Fox

RETIRED PROFESSIONAL ACTION GROUP
Elma Griesel

SMALL CLAIMS STUDY GROUP
John Weiss

CENTER FOR STUDY OF RESPONSIVE LAW
Theodore J. Jacobs

FREEDOM OF INFORMATION CLEARINGHOUSE
— — Ronald L. Plesser — — —
PRESS INFORMATION CENTER

CENTER FOR CONCERNED ENGINEERING
Ralf D. Hotchkiss

CENTER FOR AUTO SAFETY
Lowell Dodge

CLEARINGHOUSE FOR PROFESSIONAL RESPONSIBILITY
Peter J. Petkas

CORPORATE ACCOUNTABILITY RESEARCH GROUP
Mark J. Green

CONGRESS PROJECT
Robert C. Fellmeth

PUBLIC INTEREST RESEARCH GROUP*
Carl Nash
Clarence M. Ditlow III

CONSUMERS' UNION OF THE U.S. INC.
Board Member Nader

STATE AND LOCAL PUBLIC INTEREST RESEARCH GROUPS

FISHERMEN'S CLEAN WATER ACTION GROUP
David R. Zwick

*Now Nader's personal staff for his role on Consumers' Union Board of Directors of the offices, returning the friendly smiles of other press building tenants with a cold look. Sometimes smoke eddied out of an office, smelling suspiciously of marijuana. A fire broke out one day, and the Raiders explained to the firemen that they were testing a product—according to rumor, a mattress.

But, except to dedicated Naderites like John Morris of the *New York Times* and Morton Mintz of the *Washington Post,* Nader's Raiders were becoming something of a joke to Washingtonians. That attitude was fed by Raiders like Mike Kinsley who told a *Washington Post* reporter, "They'll assign you to investigate pesticides. At first you don't know pesticides from Pepsi. But they operate on the theory that it takes an innocent to see that the emperor isn't wearing any clothes." A secretary at a Washington law firm said: "One of them came in here and told me he was studying pollution in the Gulf of Mexico. Yet he didn't even know what kinds of fish swim in it. He needed a lot of help." It didn't improve the Raiders' image when Fellmeth remarked of a three-thousand-page report on California's land use policies, "We've accused half the state of bribery, and we've got the proof." This boast was hardly congruent with the description of the Raiders offered by James W. Turner, one of their leaders, as "participant scholars."

Nor did another Nader project, the Capitol Hill News Service, add any luster to the Raiders' reputations. The CHNS was set up with a grant of $40,000 from Public Citizen, the Nader catch-all, to show up the wire services by supplying information on individual congressmen to small newspapers in their districts which could not afford Washington bureaus. Five reporters were hired by Peter Gruenstein, a lawyer just out of school, at salaries of $8,000— which is considered underpayment for a typist in Washington. The five were unleashed to cover the entire Congress, with high hopes that they would blanket the country with their stories. Unfortunately, a good many newspaper editors took the reasonable attitude that if the CHNS was offering its services free, it must be selling something.

What that something was became apparent when a CHNS staffer appeared at the office of a ranking House Republican. To the congressman's administrative assistant *cum* press aide, the CHNS reporter confided that he was going to "cover two or three states in your area" and asked if he could call late every week to learn what the House member had done. "If there is something, OK," the AA said. "If the boss does something, fine. If he has a specific comment to make, fine. But I will not—this office does not —make up some drivel in the hope that it will get into the papers."

"I must admit," the CHNS reporter said, "that I'm rather green and new at something like this." Several days later he called the AA. "No," he was told, "nothing this week. The congressman's committee had no meetings this week. You know yourself that there's been no floor business of any account. It's been a light week. Call me next week." The following week, the story appeared. Recalling the incident with mixed annoyance and amusement, the AA said: "You know what that reporter wrote? 'Congressman_____did nothing last week.' "*

But the idealism of the Raiders wore thin under the abrasive effects of low pay and bad treatment. The summer interns could take their $500—if they got it, which was not always—and go back to school. But the staff Raiders, for the most part graduates of Ivy League law schools who could make many times what Nader was paying them in a full-employment-for-lawyers city like Washington, drifted away—some in anger or disgust at Nader's high-handedness and his insistence that he was always right. Harrison Welford, who participated in a Nader dissection of the Agriculture Department, took a lucrative job with Senator Philip Hart (D.-Mich.). James Turner quarreled with Nader, reportedly over strategy, and went into the consumer business for himself. John Esposito, a firebrand who denies as an absolute lie a statement ascribed to him that "you pick out the one man the people trust the most, and you attack him and destroy his credibility," got himself in trouble for disclosing Senator Edmund Muskie's double standard on air pollution.** He left Nader to work at a foundation-sponsored energy project.

Gary Sellers, who had risked conflict-of-interest charges by working simultaneously on mine safety legislation for Nader's Center for the Study of Responsive Law and Representative Phillip Burton (D.-Calif.), grew tired of Nader's compulsive telephonitis. When he complained about the 3 A.M. phone calls and told Nader to stop telephoning him after 11 P.M., he got compliance.

*CHNS must be credited with some honesty. Having polled the legislative assistants of members of the Senate on the effectiveness, integrity, and ability of the one hundred senators, it reported the finding that Vance Hartke (D.-Ind.) was considered to have the "least integrity" in that august body. Yet Hartke had not only been highly lauded in previous CHNS copy. He had also received valuable help from Ralph Nader in his reelection campaign some years before.
**Muskie, in point of fact, accepted campaign contributions from perhaps the worst polluter of Maine water, closing his eyes to this offense.

Nader, as Sellers tells it, would call at one minute to eleven, then hold forth for several hours. Sellers quit Nader to work for conservative Chairman John McClellan of the Senate Appropriations Committee for reasons which generously touched only on his inadequacies, not to mention his physical and psychological fatigue.

> You lose your capacity for outrage [he told William Greider]. If you struggle for two or three years on an issue and get your half-a-loaf, part of your honor is tied up in preserving that compromise. You have an interest in defending it. I couldn't go back to the coal-mine people and be perpetually outraged on some of those things that I had psychologically compromised on, things that I had decided were the best possible at the time.

For the Raiders who defected but remained silent when questioned by questing reporters, the real psychological fatigue came from a rejection of the Nader thesis that to prove that there was "rat shit in your frankfurters" you had to send the entire meat industry to the guillotine and, in the process, condemn yourself to a life of screaming monasticism. Of those Raiders who remained, some were motivated by a spirit of self-abnegation, however Nader might pollute Christian charity in his relationship to friend or foe. There were others who, like Donald Ross, realized that in spite of the low pay and personal crucifixion at the hands of Nader, they were ciphers without him.

The ex-Raiders have been very careful to moderate their criticisms of Nader—some out of loyalty, some out of a realization that they would pay dearly for speaking out. Fear of retribution was responsible for Nader's temporary success in concealing the Raider rebellion on the Congress Project—young people fed up with his dictatorial treatment, his utter disregard for the sensibilities of those who worked for him, and his belief that the lives of those about him were second to his demands. They could not understand why they should be relegated to outer darkness if they drank a Coke, socialized, or wanted to play softball from time to time. But most of all they resented Nader's inability to hear a point of view contrary to his, during the rare exposure they had to the "leader," or to allow them to comment on the course and direction of whatever crusade was on the agenda.

Nader's reaction to the rebellion, quickly put down, was that the Raiders couldn't "deal" with the freedom he gave them, needed "handholding," and were lazy. That their ethical sense might have been offended by such things as the Public Interest Groups he set up in the colleges could never penetrate. Those groups were financed by student activities funds to which all students are required to contribute. Nader saw nothing wrong in this. After all, he was doing "good" and that was what counted, whether or not those who were picking up the check agreed with him or not.

Nader even objected to the married life of his Raiders. "Young marriages are a problem," he told biographer McCarry. Young wives are the leading assets of corporate power. They want the suburbs, a house, a settled life. And respectability. They want society to see that they have exchanged themselves for something of value." And McCarry quotes one of the Raiders significantly:

> "Ralph always asks us how hard we work," says one of his most effective and least reverent lieutenants, "and we always lie." It is impossible for this young man to cut himself off from art and friendship and girls and sport. "Ralph is about the most *alive* guy I have ever met," says another associate. "But—Jesus!—he and I are alive in different ways." It is not that Nader is unaware of the needs of ordinary people, merely that he regards appetite as irrelevant.

Nader even objects to having his Raiders speak to the press about such problems as race and war, and he once drove one of his aides into disavowing comments he had made to a reporter on these matters. For Nader, these too are irrelevant in his war against the American business system. In Sparta, he would have been a general, and this is what the Raiders have never been able to understand, although those remaining have been able to accept it grudgingly. That he should have been able to allow Joan Claybrook, who ran his Congress Project, to dock volunteers $50 from their meager pay if their reports required rewriting is an index of the man in his relations to those who sit at his feet. It may explain the sloppiness of his Raiders and their operations.

7

Those Nader Reports

IF A MAN FROM MARS WERE TO SET DOWN HIS SPACECRAFT ON earth and devote his time to the reading of certain writings, he would be shocked to learn that it was peopled by two classes— thieves and fools. If he did not flee but remained to study the evidence, he would discover that this analysis of the earthling population, particularly those of an American persuasion, came from a small but vocal breed of prophets. And if he studied further, he would be overcome by the knowledge that these prophets did not draw their inspiration from Jeremiah or Elijah or Isaiah, but from a figure in the Book named Ananias. He might wonder why Ananias and his disciples had not been ceremoniously seated on a rail and ridden out of town, in a manner once traditional, dripping with tar and feathers. But by this time he would most certainly have lost interest in his studies and taken off on his UFO for parts unknown.

Americans are less fortunate, for they have no place to go. At every turn they are beset by the preachments of the new prophets who tell them in the unmistakable accents of Naderism that their country is foul and that they must rise up, bringing purification and a resultant utopia by destroying it. This is the message in the millions of words of a long series of reports sanctified by Ralph Nader. These reports, each one more strident and less accurate than its fellows, are the products of a children's crusade. One of them, accepted with fawning eagerness by segments of the media, was prepared by some law students, college undergraduates, and high school seniors who, unable to complete their researches before their academic doors reopened, served up their incomplete findings as the new Revelation and returned to their copy books.

This characterization of the Nader Reports, harsh as it may seem, is truly charitable when they are held up to the record. Even a would-be journalist, in the throes of his first year in journalism school, would have come to this conclusion if he had rid himself of preconceptions, antagonisms, and the vitriolic assessment of America so beloved of the Naderist muckrakers. If this sounds polemic, proof of the pudding may be found in the words of David Swankin, head of the Washington office of Consumers Union, an organization which has joined forces with Nader and contributes to the budget of a Nader satellite, the Center for Auto Safety. When the Center came up with *What To Do With Your Bad Car*, an opus known as the "Lemon Book" which has sold hundreds of thousands of copies, Consumers Union refused to publish the book. Said Swankin, "If it had been submitted as a Ph.D. thesis, a lot of our engineers would have flunked it."

Despite this acid rejection, Nader continues to accept what money he can get from Consumers Union—while pushing the sale of his lemon on bad cars. This is par for the course for Nader, who never bites the hand that contributes, yet goes along merrily befuddling the consumers whose cause he purportedly advocates. It would take a small library to take up the Nader Reports and to analyze them line by line, page by page. But it should be enough simply to survey some representative reports to demonstrate that they are a fraud perpetrated on the American people. Their shock value was great when they were issued. But the net effect has been to cast suspicion on those earnest and accurate critics of such ills as exist in the American system and to make disreputable the honest profession of muckraking.

When Nader aimed his "advocacy scholarship"—a patent contradiction in terms—at California, the director of his project gloated that "half the state" was profiting from the putative corruption of its land-use system. Elementary logic should have whispered to Nader that if 50 percent of the population had a good thing going for it, the system was hardly geared to benefit the handful of "special interest" conspirators who were his target. But it may be argued that numbers are not everything to a man who has made millions of dollars berating those who make millions of dollars. What should have been important was the accuracy of his indictment.

Power and Land in California, a 1,200-page, three-part study

of California problems, did little to generate light or even heat—
and why the Sierra Club Foundation should have pooled its resources with those of the Center for the Study of Responsive Law
to produce it is perhaps an example of the high regard in which
certain organizations hold misinformation. It was at best a compendium of old and sometimes discredited charges, seasoned with
the spice of Nader's vituperative rhetoric. As one critic pointed
out, there were no heroes in the account and not even a grudging
concession that some of those with whom the Raider authors so
passionately disagreed might conceivably be honest. California's
officialdom was corrupt, incompetent, or venal—and this blanket
charge included some of the most dedicated combatants for the
kind of conservation Nader presumably sought.

That Governor Ronald Reagan should have been a prime target
was no surprise. Nader & Company believe that Republicans
should be struck regularly, like gongs. But former Governor Edmund (Pat) Brown was assailed, without so much as a phone call
to check the validity of the charges leveled against him. So, too,
were other Democratic officials of unblemished reputation who
suddenly found themselves cast in the role of unscrupulous and
money-grubbing politicians. The report said that Brown had sold
out to large California landowners, granting them special privi-
leges when he was governor and fronting for them after he left
office.

The state legislature was dismissed as being involved in a "conflict of interest" on land issues because most of its members were
lawyers whose law firms in some instances took the cases of land
developers. This was determined by the Raiders in an interesting
way. The offices of twenty-five legislators were called by Nader
investigators. Posing as land developers—the *New York Times*
changed that to land *speculators* in the retelling—a Raider would
ask if the law firm would represent him. In eighteen cases, the girl
at the telephone said "yes"—hardly surprising since there is nothing either illegal or immoral about developing land, and everyone
under the Constitution has the right to counsel. An assent from a
secretary, however, resulted in a Raider determination that the
legislator was corrupt.

But the Raiders made a number of mistakes—understandable
since they have great difficulty in distinguishing a "yes" from a
"no." One of those charged with venality by the Raiders in this
exercise of guilt by occupation was Assemblyman Edwin L.
Z'Berg, chairman of the Assembly's Natural Resources and Con-

servation Committee, and a man widely respected for his integrity. "I do not now nor have I ever represented a land developer," Z'Berg indignantly told the press. "I can't visualize the basis for Nader's statement. I've never been approached by a land developer. They would look at me aghast." Another legislator accused of representing land developers had not practiced law for years.

It was on the basis of this kind of two-penny investigation that the Nader study stated flatly: "Land interests, to a significant extent, have bought, intimidated, compromised and supplied key officials in state and local government to a point where those interests govern the governors." And it was on the basis of this kind of shotgun blast that Henry J. Mills, head of the Metropolitan Water District of Southern California, counterattacked by describing the Nader study as "a highly irresponsible and slap-dash compilation of inaccuracies, untruth, malicious rumors, unsupported charges, distortions, and headline-hunting generalizations."

Water is a life-or-death matter in California and the Southwest. When a group of uninformed and inexperienced Raiders began sloshing about, demanding that this or that water project be scrapped because it was "the largest special interest boondoggle in history," it could be counted on to bring the kind of sharp rebuttal to which Ralph Nader was unaccustomed. And that rebuttal went straight to the point of the Nader methodology. Writing from Sacramento, where even the left-wing press was up in arms, Ernest D. Furgurson, a Scripps-Howard columnist, warned:

> The Nader report epitomizes one of the most dangerous and dishonest traits of the new generation of muckrakers: That certain truths, such as the venality of public officeholders, are taken for granted and therefore any amount of sloppiness and one-sidedness in accusations about them is forgivable, because everybody knows they are guilty anyway.
>
> Mr. Fellmeth, the head of the study, was asked why Mr. Brown and others had not been given an opportunity to reply. "I guess we probably should have confronted them," he said. "It was probably a failing on our part. This report is not the kind of document you go to court with. I know it needs more work. It contains basic, raw information."
>
> So he admits it is fallible, but goes on making it public.

Furgurson was not alone in his criticism. In the same column, he quoted Richard Rodda, political editor of the liberal *Sacramento Bee*, who had covered the Nader story from the start:

"There is not enough evidence in the hundreds of pages of charges and insinuations to convict anyone of misappropriating as much as a state-owned paper clip." The point was a good one. For if California's corporate landholders, aided by government officials, were "looting the public treasury" as the study flatly charged, then Nader and his Raiders were guilty of misprision, a felony in itself, for not reporting the crime and turning over their evidence to the proper law enforcement authorities. If they had no evidence, then they were guilty of perpetrating a fraud on the public. But most of the press, which gave wide exposure to Nader's allegations, seldom pressed him for any substantiation or told him to fish or cut bait.

United Press International, in its story on one of the press conferences Nader held to launch the California study, did note that "most of the material collected by Mr. Nader's investigators has been published and debated before" and slapped him across the wrist with: "A section is devoted to the debate over a planned Pacific Gas & Electric Co. nuclear plant at Bodega Head, north of San Francisco. The company abandoned the site more than five years ago." But it led its story with a Nader headline-grabbing prediction, paraphrased by UPI, that California "was probably going to be devastated by one or two major earthquakes in the next 20 or 30 years and that state officials were not doing enough to prepare for it."

The Nader report on New York's First National City Bank—the second largest in the country—was a comedy from beginning to end. It was issued before the "investigation" was completed because, as previously noted, some of the Raiders—including a high school senior and several college undergraduates—had to go back to their lessons. Though the bank management granted the Raiders fifty-three interviews with officials, lasting hundreds of hours, and turned over voluminous records, the Raiders complained that they had gotten "very limited" cooperation and had been thwarted by conspiratorial secrecy. In their first interview with Walter B. Wriston, Citibank's chief executive officer, they demonstrated their keen understanding of banking.

Recalling that interview, Wriston later related: "They named someone none of us had ever heard of and we asked, 'Who is he?' "

"He controls the loan policy," a Raider said. "He determines who gets the loans." Wriston patiently explained that not one but two thousand lending officers approved or disapproved loans. The Raiders continued to insist that there was a "Svengali" who was in charge. During this time, bank officials were searching for the man the Raiders had named. When he was located, it turned out that he was a loan clerk. His comment to the "investigators" was, "I don't determine nothing."

For a year—on paper at least—the Raiders ranged Citibank, looking for evidence of fraud, crime, and vicious policy. As always, they made note of what seemed damaging and ignored everything else. But so ignorant of money and financing were the Raiders that they could state in their report that Citibank "was taking money from those who can least afford to lose it and giving it to those who need it the least." On examination, it developed that, according to Raider economics, a man who deposits money in a bank "loses" it and is being victimized by the borrower who pays interest for the use of that money. A corollary to this Nader charge was one that Citibank turned away from making home loans— belied by the fact that the bank held at the time some $260 million in FHA home mortgages alone.

Another high crime of Citibank, according to the Raiders, was that it had a "symbiotic relationship" with business, which it tried to "nurture." Translated, this meant that the Citibank, which makes money by lending money, tries to see that the businesses to whom it extends credit prosper. In other words, the Raiders were arguing that Citibank was evading its social responsibilities by not scattering its money to the winds on losing ventures and perhaps going bankrupt in the process. This kind of economic thinking became apparent in an interview between Wriston and David Leinsdorf, leader of the Citibank project.

"Leinsdorf was giving me this jazz about allocating X percent to housing," says Wriston. "That's the oldest argument in the world. The king sits on the throne and says all left-handed serfs to the field, and all right-handed serfs to the laundry. Any arbitrary allocation not done by the free market is going to be destroyed the day it's done."

The Citibank study, a 406-page mouse laboriously produced by the Raiders, anguished over the callousness of a management that sued twice as many delinquent borrowers as any other New York Bank—but failed to mention that it makes almost four times as many personal loans as its four major competitors put together. Its major recommendations were that the Justice Department should investigate Citibank for possible violations of the antitrust statutes and for failure to serve summonses properly to customers in default, that labor unions should organize Citibank employees, and that the bank should give its customers better service.

The Nader report on Citibank hardly set the financial community on fire. And the bank officials, instead of cowering or apologizing, struck back. Said the rebuttal:

> It is difficult to know how to respond to a 500-page report which is on both sides of many issues.
>
> For example, we are alleged to have abandoned the tax-exempt bond market on one page, while our preference for tax-exempt securities is given as our reason for supporting the World Trade Center on another page.
>
> We are told that our record of credit extension is "very good" in one breath, but that our craving for growth has led us to condone sloppy credit procedures in another.
>
> We are accused of shoveling funds to our corporate customers at the expense of the small consumer, while at the same time we are supposed to be foisting unwanted credit on the poor.
>
> We are blamed in one breath for failing to help the City of New York deal with its massive problems, and in the next castigated for permitting our officers to serve on municipal and regional groups attempting to work on those problems . . .
>
> We will be glad to respond to either position, but it is impossible to respond to both.

The Nader report on the Civil Service Commission, a 500-page document replete with the usual charges of "bureacratic lawlessness," was an excellent example of the publicity end run. Through the Nader espionage apparatus in the government, the Raiders learned that the commission was preparing a monumental study of its workings, with a view to the improvement of procedures. A task force under Raider Robert Vaughn was set up to beat the CSC to the punch with its criticisms. The Raiders were welcomed by CSC officials until it became evident that they were not interested in facts but in a hatchet job. As CSC chairman Robert E. Hampton reported to the Congress after the Nader report had been issued:

> During the fact-finding phase, in contacts with Commission staff —by lines of questioning, display of attitudes and biases, and out-of-hand rejection of reasonable responses to many questions—it was evident that conclusions were cast in concrete before we were visited. In fact . . . the Nader team stated that their study methology started with preconceptions, and followed up with a search for findings to support these preconceptions. Needless to say, as a re-

search methodology, this approach is certainly unprofessional, if not unethical.

The report was unprofessional in many other ways. Much of what it recommended, based on CSC studies of the agency, had already been put into effect. The "facts" on which other recommendations seemed based were substantiated usually by horror stories attributed to anonymous sources. The report dished up the novel theory that civil service workers were not sufficiently protected in their jobs, though precisely the opposite has been a chronic complaint in Washington from people who have been subjected to incompetent or arrogant treatment at the hands of Federal employees who cannot be touched. *Spoiled System*, Nader's idea of wit in titling the report, came up with a typical solution to the problems created by a ballooning bureaucracy—more bureaucracy. It recommended that certain CSC functions be taken out of the hands of the commissioners and entrusted to still another agency—an independent Employees Rights and Accountability Board with quasi-judicial powers to hear grievances and eliminate "abuses." Why and how a new body could succeed where the CSC had allegedly failed was not evident in the report —nor could it be since the experience of government has always been that every new agency merely creates problems of its own.

The Nader report on the CSC attempted to flog the issue of equal opportunity. But when it demanded that the CSC should increase the representation of women and minority group members on its Bureau of Personnel Investigations, it was not aware that of the twenty-five most recently hired persons in BPI, fourteen came from minority groups. The report further charged that the Equal Opportunity program was inadequate because it was run by whites, an accusation which conveniently overlooked the fact that the director of that program was a black and that others—such as the directors of the Spanish Speaking Program and the Women's Program—had been recruited from the appropriate minority.

If the response to the Nader report of the Civil Service Commission was one big yawn, *Damming the West*, on the Bureau of Reclamation, was met with anger and ridicule for its institutionalized ignorance. Waving the bloody rag, the Nader team's study, written by three eastern law students, charged that BuRec projects "waste billions of dollars, damage the environment and benefit only a handful of farmers, politicians, and bureaucrats." This criticism of programs which put thirty-three million acres of arid land under cultivation in seventeen states and gave them a crop value of almost two billion dollars in 1969 alone—and which supplied forty-nine power plants with a capacity of 7.4 million kilowatts and an income of $140 million—was, as Felix Sparks, the director of the Colorado Water Conservation Board, said, "typical Nader." Without the Bureau of Reclamation, many millions of Americans would lose their livelihood. Arizona would die and the lush valleys of California would return to desert land. BuRec, moreover, was one government agency which was returning to the United States Treasury, at an ongoing rate, the $6.2 billion invested in its activities.

What the Nader report on BuRec demonstrated conspicuously was that the Raiders knew nothing about reclamation and nothing about agriculture, but a great deal about making headlines. To prove the uselessness of reclamation projects and bolster the argument that BuRec was putting people out of business, *Damming the West* noted that cotton acreage in the South had dropped by one third in a twenty-year period, whereas cotton acreage in the Southwest had increased 300 percent. Much of that Southwestern cotton, the report stated portentously, was shipped to cotton mills in the South. What the Raiders did not know is that the Southwest produces long-staple cotton which would have had to be imported from Egypt and other countries. The South grows short-staple cotton, and cotton mills need both types.

According to the Nader report, sugar beet production on BuRec lands should be curtailed because it costs the taxpayer $19 million annually in Sugar Act payments. This, of course, was false. Since 1934, all Treasury payments under the Sugar Act exceeded all expenditures by $600 million.

Said the Nader report: "Perhaps as many as 180,000 farm workers have been driven from their jobs as a result of BuRec's shortsighted policies." The answer to this, of which the Nader task force could not have been unaware, was that since 1944, farm employment has dropped by some five million as a result of increased farm efficiency, which saw one farm worker supplying the needs of forty-five people whereas three decades ago he could only supply the needs of thirteen people. In the outcry over *Damming the West*, moreover, farm experts and other authorities noted that impact studies had demonstrated that BuRec projects generated employment.

Said the report: "Between 1960 and 1969, over 1.4 million fish perished in several massive fish kills because of Bureau of Reclamation's failure to maintain adequate water conditions." Those fish kills, however, were the result of discharges of industrial waste and domestic sewage over which BuRec has no control. The report attacked the Central Arizona Project, arguing that it should be stopped because it was a boondoggle and asserting that it would raise the cost of water by 1,000 percent—a statistic manufactured out of the whole cloth. Point after point, some simple and some complex, raised by Nader's Raiders turned out to be captious or false. The effect was not merely to destroy the credibility of Ralph Nader and his colleagues. It also inspired a serious question: Why had an agency like the Bureau of Reclamation been singled out for destructive attack? Was Nader running out of targets?

Continuing to strike, Nader's Raiders took on the Veterans Administration. Nader had said on the Dick Cavett Show that the "indifference and waste in . . . the bureaucracy in the federal government dealing with veterans affairs is really colossal" and would make an "unbelievable study." Thereupon a Raider task force was set up consisting of a young nonveteran, who worked at it between attending classes at Harvard, and a number of part-time assistants, who endeavored to analyze instantly the third largest agency in the government with the second largest budget. These earnest seekers after truth never even bothered to interview the head of the Veterans Administration, and they came up with the recommendation that veterans' pensions should be discontinued. They also charged that the VA discriminated against Vietnam veterans even though the agency was hiring them at the rate of a thousand a month.

But while Nader was busy trying to destroy one government bureaucracy in order to replace it with one of his own choosing, he was not being unfaithful to his first hate—American industry. It is not difficult to understand why, in an attempt to find himself another Corvair, Nader chose the E. I. du Pont de Nemours & Co. —DuPont, the great chemical giant. DuPont was big, DuPont was successful, DuPont was an asset to the American economic system, and DuPont—by paying high wages and treating its employees well—had been able to keep Big Labor out. DuPont, however, operated out of a small state and could be depicted as an industrial octopus dominating every facet of that state's life. On that last point, DuPont was a sitting duck. Of course, the company had power in Delaware. The question to an objective observer would have been, how is that power used? But even before his gaggle of graduate students had begun their three-month study, the question had been answered and Nader was ready to pull all the stops. Among those stops was the imputation that DuPont was anti-Semitic even though the vice president assigned to work with the Raiders was named Irving Shapiro. From the start of their investigation, the Raiders also began to lay the groundwork for their charge that the company did not cooperate—as if there were a federal law that it must—by demanding access to company records which would not have been available to the attorney-general of the United States without a court order.

The Company State was the title given to the Nader study of DuPont, and its direction can best be described by quoting from the *Washington Post* summation:

> A team of Ralph Nader's associates has labeled Delaware a "company state" where officers of the E. I. du Pont de Nemours & Co. and members of the large du Pont family control virtually every facet of social and economic life.
> In a two-volume study of the du Pont Co.'s "pervasive" and "decisive" control over Delaware, the Nader group alleged that the nation's 18th largest industrial corporation does not pay its fair share of taxes, condones racism in its hometown of Wilmington, and prevents dissent through its ownership of the state's two major newspapers . . .

The catalogue of DuPont transgression was long, through all the passions ranging. The company was accused of being a shameless polluter, of using its money for charitable purposes which Nader Raiders did not find to their liking, of not having blacks on its board of directors, of encouraging its employees to take part in civic affairs in order to dominate local government, of imposing a low corporate tax rate on the state, thereby benefiting. It found as an example of venality the help that the then chairman of the board, Lammot du Pont Copeland, gave to his son, noting that the Wilmington Trust bank made a loan to Copeland Jr. of $3,718,925 —a loan not difficult to understand since it was secured by half a million dollars in collateral, with $3,350,000 personally guaranteed by Copeland Sr. That fifty other banks not in Delaware had been ready to lend Copeland Jr. money was seen as a somehow suspicious circumstance.

As usual, the eager Raiders tended to get their facts wrong, but never so wrong that an error favorable to DuPont or the members of the du Pont family might slip in. And in the slam-bam-thank-you-mam of the report, the Delaware Study Group demonstrated, as Melvin J. Grayson and Thomas R. Shepard Jr., two former *Look* magazine executives, noted in their *The Disaster Lobby,* that "it knew nothing about big business and had decided in advance that the company was wrong."

> A careful examination of the report reveals the lengths to which the Nader group went to put DuPont in a bad light. For example, at one point the study team is sharply critical of a member of the du Pont family for having avoided the payment of inheritance taxes by leaving the bulk of his estate to a charitable foundation. Later on in the study, the company is denounced for its failure to contribute to charity the full 5 percent of net income it is permitted to deduct for tax purposes. "In other words," noted a DuPont executive, "we were damned if we did and damned if we didn't."

But it was worse than that. DuPont was criticized for having selected a private local organization as an aid to minority businesses rather than a governmental body. In point of fact, the organization was not selected by DuPont but by the black community. DuPont was charged with having evaded its responsibilities in pollution control and with having spent microscopic amounts of money to that end. The facts were that DuPont had spent $207 million on pollution control at the time the report was written, with another $600 million pledged. And it had put in the equivalent of 1,300 employees, working full time, to anti-pollution work.

DuPont was accused of using its influence over the state legislature to create a tax structure which allowed it to bilk the taxpayer and favor itself and the rich. Actually, Delaware has the highest rate of personal income tax of any state in the union. And its corporate tax was 2.2 percentage points higher than the national average. In order to prove that the du Ponts were not paying their share of real estate taxes, the Raiders had to develop what they conceded was a "novel" way of computing the right amount of taxes—an arcane system called "assessment per unit of size" nowhere recognized by tax experts. Efforts to keep down the amount of heavy industry in the state was seen by the Raiders as a means of not having to share "the open sewer" of the Delaware River with other businesses. That DuPont gave its employees up to 20 percent time off to work in government was interpreted as a sinister plot.

77

But the lowest blow of all was struck at former Senator John J. Williams, a Delaware Republican who, as Clark Mollenhoff, one of the most tenacious investigative reporters in the country, would write, "was busy crusading for the American taxpayer for nearly twenty years before Nader arrived on the Washington scene." Known as "the conscience of the Senate," Williams had on a number of occasions opposed DuPont, even though his constituency was "the company state" which, the Raiders claimed, ruled its politicians with an iron hand, and he had done so where billions of dollars were at stake. Nevertheless, Williams was accused by the Raiders of doing for DuPont "essentially what he has been accusing Bobby Baker for"—a rank libel since Baker had gone to prison for the misuse of campaign money, defrauding the government of great sums, and evading his income taxes.

The basis for this character assassination was an amendment to a general revenue bill, introduced by Williams, which allowed those whose property had been seized in the Communist takeover of Cuba to to write this off in their income taxes. The Williams legislation, which had been approved by the Treasury Department of a Democratic administration, had the unanimous support of the Senate Finance Committee. The Raiders, however, implied that Williams had introduced his amendment as part of a secret deal made with illegally unregistered DuPont lobbyists to protect $1.6 million of DuPont money. But, as Mollenhoff wrote, "the DuPont claim was only one of 7,659 individual claims with a total value of $490,413,000. The DuPont claim amounted to less than one-half of one percent of the total . . . The explanation by Senator Williams of the 1964 tax bill is supported fully by the records of the Senate Finance Committee and the *Congressional Record* for that time."

Nader, whose name was emblazoned on the cover of *The Company State* in letters far larger than those of its putative authors, seemed to have no compunctions about attempting to destroy the reputation of a universally honored civil servant who in his lifetime had saved the American taxpayer billions of dollars. Yet Mollenhoff was one of the few in the media who set the record straight. The rest of those who gave columns of copy to the Nader report on Delaware either dutifully accepted what Nader and the Raiders had charged or glossed it over.

There were other equally inaccurate, misinformed, preconceived, and opinionated reports by Nader and the Raiders, all foisted on the public as the result of meticulous research by dedicated consumer advocates and battlers for the commonweal. Ironically, the net effect of the seemingly unending stream of Nader exposés was to discourage the kind of muckraking which had served the nation so well in the populist era at the turn of the century, encouraging a bored cynicism at every new outburst of indignation by the Raiders. A conscientious critic of existing flaws in the American system knew that the decibel level of a Nader attack could never be matched by those who respected the facts and sought reform on the basis of what was truly unjust.

But the moment of truth was to come later when Nader, in a fit of pique at the Congress of the United States, decided to punish it for not accepting his every word, his every charge of criminal behavior, as having been writ on stone and brought down from the mountain top.

8

Giving Congress
the Business

HUNCHED OVER THE LECTERN BEFORE A LUNCHEON AUDIENCE-
at the National Press Club, Ralph Nader made what he considered
a momentous announcement. He was launching, Nader told the
assembled members of the Washington press corps, "what is probably the most comprehensive and detailed study of the Congress
since its establishment." With typical modesty he ignored the 144
card-file drawers in the Library of Congress on the subject of his
investigation, as well as many shelves of books by political scientists and journalists examining the workings of the national legislature in minute detail.

> The non-partisan Congress Project will enlist the assistance of hun-
> dreds of citizens covering nearly every Congressional District
> [Nader said]. Here in Washington about 80 graduate students and
> young professionals will conduct research during portions of this
> year-long study . . . It will range from an analysis of the electoral and
> campaign process to individual profiles of members of Congress to
> the internal workings of the legislature and its interaction with the
> Executive Branch and private constituencies. The study's purpose
> will be to concentrate on dynamic and internal forces, to diagnose
> deficiencies, record strengths and recommend the ways and means
> of effecting the desired changes based on past experience of the
> Congress and future prospects for reform.
>   . . . For some of Washington's old hands, this aspiration may be
> taken as bad humor if not explicitly bizarre. But if one considers the
> number of flexible and decentralized options and authorities avail-
> able to Congress perhaps it is easier to conclude that the importance
> of being Congress far transcends its endemic delay and chronic

inaction which its insulated surroundings have woven into its fabric. Certainly many previous studies, including some by former members, serve to confirm this observation.

If information is the currency of democracy, it is time to apply that principle to the sinews of citizenship involvement with their representatives in Congress. Who is to say that our Congressmen and Senators would not welcome the participation of the people [in this investigation].

Few in the audience on that early November 1971 afternoon took Nader's announcement seriously. The more cynical among them saw it as a typical Nader response to the growing resistance on Capitol Hill to his histrionics. And even the youngest and newest of the newspapermen present was aware of the vast and subtle complexities of the congressional system—its organization, the interplay of personal and political forces, the accretion of rights and subterfuges, the sometimes Byzantine interaction of executive and legislative power, the traditions which have more force than law in its everyday workings. Nader proponents saw the Congress Project as a prod to reform which, even in failure, would have impact if only by the threat of its existence.

As usual, the cynics were the closest to the truth. For the Congress Project, conceived in secrecy in the basement of a Washington office building months before, was meant as a rebuke to a Senate and House which would not bow to Nader's direction or accept as Revelation his blueprint for the totalitarian American society he had conceived. The secrecy in which the project had been planned was, in a sense, a tacit admission of its punitive nature. As one of Nader's adjutants told *National Journal*, "Not even the rest of the Raider operation was supposed to know about it. Ralph had a lot of irons in the fire on the Hill which he didn't want to upset by setting off a lot of paranoia about Nader raiding the Hill." This was a far cry from the anticipated gratitude in Congress that he had suggested in his National Press Club address.

There were, of course, other motivating factors. The staggering scope of the inquiry, its grandiosity, appealed to Nader's growing sense of power. It was so important to him that he was ready to back it with a half-million dollars of his "own" money. All other Nader activities were thrust aside, even his brooding concern over the fat content of hamburger meat, and the whole chaotic machinery of research and propaganda was put to work on the task ahead. It was go for broke. "Somebody can say that this will be a study that will lose support for various programs in the Congress," Nader told a reporter. "It doesn't make any difference . . . Congress has become so impotent that there's nothing left of any expectation beyond what it's been doing . . . We don't need Congress."

This much could be said for the Congress Project. Experts had covered the ground before, but no one had ever attempted to do it all at once—and with raw recruits who, as researchers, hardly knew one end of a questionnaire from the other. After the preparation of innumerable memoranda interminably discussed, the project focused on twenty-two areas, each to be mapped in a 3,000-page study—fact-crammed, to the point, and written in a style which would arouse the great American public and involve it in something more important that the evening's television fare. Among these areas were:

The American Vision of Congress, dealing with the myths and realities of Congress as seen by the country and by itself.

Apportionment and Voting Rights, a study of redistricting.

Campaign Finance, on the laws and techniques of funding the electoral process.

Incumbency and Competition, on the advantages of those holding office who are challenged at reelection time.

In the Committees, a study of how committees function.

After the Committees: How a Bill Becomes Law, a study of procedures and abuses.

In the Washington Web: An Ethnography, an inquiry into the social patterns of Washington and how they exert pressure on the Congress.

Information Sources and the Legislature, a study on how Congress gets the facts on which it bases legislation.

Entangled in the Web: Conflict of Interest, a study of the conflicts between a legislator's duty and his own natural or purchased predilections.

Party Politics, the interaction of party organizations and the congressional leadership.

Who Represents America, profiles of House and Senate members to determine if they really represent America, a composite study.

This "most comprehensive and detailed study" of the Congress was to be released by January 1973, in what could only be described as instant pyramid-building. Despite the tremendous expenditure of money and effort—the sweat and tears of an underpaid corps of researchers—the reports were never issued, nor is there any indication that they ever will be. For the major thrust of the Congress Project, as it developed, was still another "study" —profiles of the 484 members of the House and Senate seeking reelection in 1972, which was issued some four weeks before Election Day—and a scissors-and-paste paperback, *Who Runs Congress?,* dashed off by three writers in a matter of weeks, with no relation to the massive studies presumably under way at the time.

It was the profiles, however, which tore the Nader trousers from Genesis to Revelations and may have forever destroyed his effectiveness as people's lawyer, consumer advocate, and anointed of God. For the first instrument of torture devised by Nader and his Raiders was the questionnaire—633 questions which, with subquestions, amounted to almost a thousand queries. Some of the questions were sophomoric. Others, if answered, would have put the respondents in jeopardy with their colleagues, for Nader was in effect asking them to tattle on each other. Even income tax returns were demanded. By a conservative estimate, moreover, if all those queried had answered the questionnaire in full, it would have taken up close to a million dollars of congressional time.*

The questionnaires, moreover, were to be followed by personal interviews, also disruptive of congressional time. In effect, Nader was asking the Congress to put aside all its business while the Raiders—in time they reached the staggering number of 1,250— poked into its personal affairs, rummaged through its files, unburied the confidences of constituents, and—in several notable

*It is interesting that, though Nader and Congress Project director Robert Fellmeth wanted the full attention of the entire Congress, neither of them had the time to sign the letters they sent Congress. An examination of the various letters, several in number, shows obviously different signatures on each of them for Nader and Fellmeth. (See page 85.)

cases—sought out the details of the sex lives of members who refused to cooperate. Had the questions being asked been searching and knowledgeable, there might have been some rationale for them. But political scientists at the Brookings Institution, Johns Hopkins University, and elsewhere took one look at them and shuddered. Even a tame psychologist hired by Nader to study what answers were received threw up his hands and said they would be worthless in any attempt at an evaluation of congressional caliber. But Nader rode roughshod over these protests and ordered full steam ahead.

Normally, an invasion such as that of the Raiders would have been thrown bodily off Capitol Hill. But there was an implicit threat which some congressmen, particularly those with liberal constituencies, could not ignore. It was a power play on Nader's part. This was made explicit by Michael Pertschuk, then chief counsel of the Senate Commerce Committee, who had worked hand and glove with Nader. "He's got to knock off a couple of congressmen," Pertschuk told Paul Leventhal of *National Journal.* "It all comes down to power. Then they'll pay attention to him. It's not relevant whether his friends are mad at him. Or even whether he has a reputation for total accuracy. What counts is his impact on the electoral process. That's a fairly cynical view, but I think valid nonetheless." The menace lurked in the very broad hint that those who did not fully cooperate would be stigmatized for having something to hide.*

Much of the suspicion on Capitol Hill stemmed from a realization that Nader's "most comprehensive" study of the Congress was simply window dressing for the politically explosive profiles. That Nader wanted them in print and on sale before the November election—at no matter what cost—seemed the giveaway of his motivation. And his attempts at mollifying the Congress and allaying its fears backfired badly. Several meetings were scheduled at

*An evaluation by Nader of the questionnaires would have involved a conflict of interest. Senator Gaylord Nelson (D.-Wisc.) is a director of Nader's Center for Auto Safety. Another director of the Center is Representative Benjamin Rosenthal (D.-N.Y.). Among the Senate staff which has been part of the "Nader network" are James F. Flug, Senator Edward M. Kennedy's chief counsel on a Judiciary subcommittee; Senator Philip A. Hart's assistant counsel on another Judiciary subcommittee; the aforementioned Michael Pertschuk, on Senator Warren Magnuson's Commerce Committee; Kenneth A. McLean, professional staff consultant on Senator John Sparkman's Senate Banking Committee; and Martin Lobel, Senator William Proxmire's legislative assistant. What, it may be asked, would Nader's reaction have been if it had been discovered that these men had close ties with, let us say, General Motors or United States Steel?

Sincerely,

[signature: Ralph Nader]

Ralph Nader

[signature: Robert C. Fellmeth]

Robert C. Fellmeth
Project Director

Letter, undated

Sincerely yours,

[signature: Nader]

Ralph Nader

[signature: R. Fellmeth]

Robert C. Fellmeth
Project Director

Letter of 7 June 1972

Sincerely,

[signature: Nader]

Ralph Nader

[signature: R. Fellmeth]

Robert Fellmeth

Letter of June 29, 1972

**Varying Signatures on Letters
(See footnote, page 83)**

85

which Nader could explain his purposes to groups of legislators, and none of them went very well. But the most disastrous was his appearance before the strongly left Democratic Study Group, which thirty House members attended. Before the festivities began, Nader had the group on his side. By the time the meeting broke up, he had lost most of them, some permanently. The consensus was that Nader had been "arrogant" and "inflexible." As one member put it, "He didn't try to persuade. He just told us flatly what he wanted, with the implication that we'd better comply—or else."

Had the Nader interviewers been properly briefed—and had they understood the questions they were asking—some of the antagonism might have washed away. But with a few notable exceptions, the interviewers were obviously floundering, expecting to get their education in congressional matters from the three and four hours of interviews they exacted from interviewees. Some hid behind hostility and rudeness, but others frankly confessed their ignorance. In either case, the members felt that they were wasting their time and energy.

Emphasis on the profiles instead of the widely heralded study had its repercussions with the Nader organization. Two of the original five staff members quit in "friendly" disagreement. Others on the Congress Project who were willing to work at sweatshop wages and live in an old and non-air-conditioned George Washington University dormitory because they thought they would be doing important work, grumbled that they had been assigned a job of gossip-column reporting. But they quickly learned that they were part of a paramilitary organization—theirs not to reason why —in which orders from a commander-in-chief they almost never saw were not to be questioned. The actual writers of the profiles, each one assigned eleven of them to be turned out in a few week's time, learned that the Nader organization was run on a piece-work and speed-up system.

When the writers began missing deadlines, worn out by twelve- and fourteen-hour days of wrestling with the disorganized mass of notes, statistics, clippings, and other material dumped on their desks, Joan Claybrook, the profiles director, tacked up a notice on the bulletin board that they would be docked $50 for each profile that had to be reassigned. This caused a revolt in the ranks and added to the chaos. Claybrook attempted to quiet it by reducing the number of profiles expected of each writer to eight before the

$50 fine was exacted, but eventually Nader had to be called in to read the writers a stern lecture on their duty to the cause and to reduce the required number of profiles to six. But morale remained low, and was not improved by the disappearance from the research library of needed volumes or the "effiency" which required project workers to sign up a week in advance for the use of the office WATS telephone line. With the Congress Project steadily growing in size and numbers, the confusion was compounded.

There was another and more serious crisis in mid-July when, out of the blue, Nader announced to the troops, through what amounted to an order of the day, that a quickie paperback on the Congress was about to be produced. Said his "statement of purpose":

> Our intent is to draft a short, lucid and readable book for the average citizen. While it is essential that our group continue to produce the kind of detailed, weighty tomes for professional audiences that we have historically turned out, it is also essential that we take our message to the masses.

The "lucid and readable book" was to be turned out by three of his full-time Raiders—James M. Fallows, Mark Green, and David R. Zwick—who would do the research and writing on this inconsequential by-blow of what had been touted as a serious research effort in the space of three weeks. When Congress Project study team leaders refused to turn over material to the paperback trio, independent research had to be included in the brief period of time allowed to the book. Such an effort, coming from anyone but Ralph Nader, would have been laughed out of existence, but Nader's hardback publisher, Richard Grossman, and Bantam Books were joining together for a 500,000 first printing, agreeing with Nader that it would be a big money maker. In breaking the story of the paperback, *National Journal* reported:

> Fallows, who is the writing member of the paperback's three coauthors, said: "Ralph tried really hard to rally cooperation (of the team leaders). He held a couple of meetings to explain. But it ended in stalemate."
>
> "Ralph's session with us made it even worse," said David E. Price, 31, a political science professor at Yale, who heads the Commerce

Committee study. "It was press-conference style—40 people packed in a room. It's his way of dealing with a crisis. There was no question the project had been decided on. He just answered questions justifying the decision."

All criticism of the book was brushed aside by Nader with the *ad hominem* slur that it was motivated by "author's territoriality." But the damage had been done, and where it hurt the most— among the young people who would return to school and community with a tarnished image of the man they had idolized. And this was borne out after the profiles and the paperback, *Who Runs Congress?*, had appeared. Claudia Townsend, news editor of the University of Georgia paper, the *Red and Black*, told a Scripps-Howard reporter, "I would say I have less confidence now in the things Nader has done. The pressure and the hurry to get things done and get a report out is what helped me change my mind. I'm inclined to believe that is the way they operate all the time." What she did for Nader, she added, was "a job any 10th grader could do." Anna Zill, the pro-McGovern liberal who had written his profile, felt that Nader had "made some bad judgment decisions" and that he was "not a good chooser of his lieutenants," who were chosen because of their loyalty to him and not for their competence. She found Nader's views on the government "simplistic" and disagreed with his idea that "lawyers should run everything."

Daniel Taubman wrote a long and critical appraisal of the Congress Project for the *Harvard Law Review* in which he described the "errors of miscalculation," the "poor planning," and the general inhumanity of the treatment accorded the profile writers and the rest of the staff.

> Nader, who had previously termed the profile requirements unalterable, and then changed them, again switched horses in midstream, deciding that a short book should be written not as an overview of Congress, but as a teaser to induce citizens to buy later, more detailed studies . . .
>
> Most topics and committees researchers felt the quickie book was a transparent device for . . . grab[bing] the spotlight . . .
>
> During this mini-crisis, Nader met with [project] members in an attempt to mollify them. As he had kept his ground with profile writers, so too with the . . . researchers: We are writing a quickie book, that's that. Now, does anyone have any questions.
>
> "It was as if Mount Rushmore had crumbled," a Harvard Law

student said after attending the meeting. The students' image of Nader had been shattered.

Before the publication of the profiles and *Who Runs Congress?*, there had been some charge and countercharge between the Naderites and their victims. One tearful girl researcher had accused Representative John L. McMillan (D.-S.C.) of having told her to "get the hell out of his office" and that he was the only person who knew anything about his congressional payroll. McMillan denied the rudeness and pointed out that he could not have made the statement about his payroll because, "as everyone knows, all congressional payrolls are public records." Senator James Eastland (D.-Miss.), chairman of the powerful Judiciary Committee, reported that he had been approached in a Senate corridor by a researcher seeking an interview who had never showed up. On the other hand, one Raider had told a reporter that in interviewing Senator J. William Fulbright, he had been "too intimidated" to ask him about his anti-civil rights record.

But when the book and the profiles made their appearance, just before the election of November 1972, they proved to be yawn-provokers. For the most part, they were met by amusement and ridicule on the part of both the Congress and the press covering Capitol Hill. Here and there, a Hill correspondent would explode with indignation. One veteran correspondent called them "a goddam outrage, a scissors-and-paste job," and "shabby work." But the electorate showed little interest and only the lobbyists hustled to buy the profiles in hopes of finding something of value about the personal lives of specific members of Congress. Lobbyists could, of course, afford the $40 price tag on a complete set of profiles.

Newspaper stories on the profiles were hardly rhapsodic. They consisted in detailing the many errors of fact called to the attention of reporters by maligned members and to pointing out the obvious bias. Typical of the latter was a review by Mary Russell of the *Washington Post* which noted that in dealing with Representative Chet Holifield, who had tangled with Nader, the profile had emphasized his "refusal" to cooperate, whereas Senator McGovern was said to be "unable" to do so. (*Time* said of the McGovern profile that it was "so uncritical as to seem reverential.")

In a story for the *Washington Star-News*, Shirley Elder and Dana Bullen made the point even plainer:

Despite the aim of even-handedness, some of the profiles reflect the bias one might expect from an army of idealistic volunteers new to politics and dedicated to reforming the system.

Writer Robert Schwartzman was easy on Senator Edward M. Kennedy, for instance, ignoring a college exam cheating incident and making only passing reference to the auto accident at Chappaquiddick that took a girl's life and has never been fully explained.

But the Ku Klux Klan background of West Virginia's Senator [Robert] Byrd is treated fully, leaving the reader with the suspicion that Byrd never really abandoned his philosophical ties with the Klan.

This bias often affected the accuracy of the profiles. In his *Chicago Tribune* column, Willard Edwards, with the experience of his great seniority in the Washington press corps, singled out one gross instance which had led Representative Robert McClory, an Illinois Republican, to characterize it as "a product of sloppy research—grossly inaccurate, unfair, offensive, misleading, and politically motivated." Underscoring that quotation, Edwards wrote:

> The young woman compiler of this report revealed her animus in an opening summary which accused McClory of publicly voicing support of issues but not "putting his vote where his voice is."
>
> To support this charge, she recorded incorrectly 50 percent of McClory's committee votes; distorted the meaning of floor amendments which he supported or opposed, and ignored his explanation (in eight hours of patient responses to her questions) of the reasons why he voted as he did.
>
> In an astonishing infraction of the "nonpartisan" spirit claimed by Nader, she sought out McClory's badly defeated Democratic opponent in the 1970 elections and liberally quoted his aspersions on the incumbent. Then she described the superior qualities of his 1972 Democratic opponent in ecstatic terms.
>
> The errors even extended to falsification of McClory's voting attendance, which was given as lower-than average. His actual attendance was 88 percent—highest of any Illinois Republican.*

McClory was only one of many members of Congress so treated, but this did not come as a surprise. Theodore Jacobs, Nader's closest associate, had, according to United Press International, said

*The AFL-CIO, Edwards reported, promptly poured additional funds into the district. Nader reports on candidates were similarly used in many other cases.

that the profiles would be published before the elections so voters would use them "to depose regressive legislators and demand reform as the price for support." Representative Edwin B. Forsythe (R.-N.J.) was accused of having voted *in favor* of a two-year extension of the draft in 1971, whereas he had voted *against* it. "My staff brought this to the attention of Mr. Nader's staff people," Forsythe wrote in *Nation's Business*, "some two months before the final profile was published. Yet they failed to make the correction." Why the votes in committee of members of the House Education and Labor Committee and the analysis of the issues involved were false or misleading became clear when a Nader Raider admitted that instead of making its own tabulation and analysis, the Nader team had "borrowed" them from the Democratic Study Group.*

But if the profiles were shoddy, *Who Runs Congress?* was an outright fraud. It was presented to the public as the result of the "most comprehensive" survey of the national legislature, whereas it was the result of the most superficial and hasty research. Whatever the faults of Congress, and they are many, it hardly merited the assertion found in the first chapter that "Few Congressmen would admit that they can be 'bought,' but their protest is like that of a free-living woman who decides she might as well take money for what she enjoys, but insists she is not a prostitute." This kind of vicious vulgarity might be forgiven someone who had made a long study of the national legislature. But the three young men who wrote the sentence, with Nader's blessing, could no more substantiate the charge than they could find their way about one of the House office buildings.

The contradictions in the book were legion. At one point, the authors conceded that for "all its flaws, Congress is the most responsive and open branch of government." At another they scolded that "Congress is only rarely accountable to the people." Again, the book could state that "Across the range of ideologies, from conservatives . . . to liberals . . . fourteen-hour days are common." Then some pages later, as Representative Clarence Long—at least once referred to as "Clem"—noted in a review for the *Maryland Law Review*, it could describe "the proud lords of legislation" as people who "frolic in the pool, sleep quietly at their desks." Long was twice described as a "former" representative,

*"If Mr. Nader had been subject to any 'truth in advertising' test, he would have failed," Forsythe wrote.

but the Nader experts also referred to John McClellan, one of the most powerful men in the Senate, as a member of the House. At one and the same time, Congress was criticized for not spending enough money on staff and for spending too much for same. The casual reader was left with the impression that the Congress was wasting the taxpayer's substance in junketing trips abroad, though this made up one-half of 1 percent of the congressional budget.

The Nader study brushed off Congress as the "great American default," the "broken branch," and argued that it was led around by the nose by the Executive Branch—"a Congress which does not lead, but is led." In another day, this characterization might have had some validity. But the Nader account was presumably describing the 93rd Congress, which opposed the President more consistently than any other Congress in more than a dozen years. Is it any wonder, then, that *Time* put aside its consistent pro-Nader slant to state that "Nearly everything but Nader's intent is wrong about this book . . . It is tendentious, hostile and superficial, and contains nary a footnote to indicate its source," and characterized the Congress Project as "marred by unsubstantiated innuendoes and unconcealed bias."

Nader's earlier reports had received reverential media attention because they dealt with subjects about which reporters knew little. *Who Runs Congress?* dealt with an institution with which the Washington press corps had daily contact. Its disillusion, therefore, was twice as great as it normally would have been because the press had a sinking feeling that it had been victimized by Nader. Those who had written of him uncritically, who had seen in him something new on the Washington scene, were forced to reexamine their premises and to look at their hero with a somewhat jaundiced eye. They had to admit that Terence Finn, legislative assistant to the liberal former senator from Maryland, Joseph Tydings, had a legitimate and telling point to make in his review of *Who Runs Congress?* in the *Washington Post's* book section:

> Consumer and environmentalist lobbies are "public" interest groups. The authors assume their good guys are the good guys and vice versa. [The book] does not ask if the education lobby's emphasis on higher education at the expense of vocational training, or the health lobby's emphasis on medical research instead of caring for patients, is in the "public" interest. But it does state what is surely questionable, that lobbies "control" the flow of information to and from Congress.

The three authors . . . have forgotten that Congress, as a representative body, is a forum of competing interests in American society. Public policy is in part the result of the consequent conflict . . . That some go unrepresented . . . doesn't justify naming one's own interests the national interest.

Furthermore, it is simplistic to argue that effective interest groups are those with money while the poor and needy lack representation. The rejection of the SST, the inability of organized labor to repeal 14(b), and the rise of the consumer movement suggest that money alone will not carry the day in Congress. Organization, popular support, the issue itself, and an understanding of the legislative process all count for much in lobbying members of Congress.

For Ralph Nader, surrounded by devils and conspiracies, Finn's logic was meaningless. Congress had stood in his way, and he had sought to smash it. "He's begun to think he's God," Senator Abraham Ribicoff had said of him. In his Congress Project, he was the God that failed. And from that moment on, his effectiveness —and the unprecendented license he had been given to berate and insult the Congress—ended. From that point on, he was no longer feared, and in time was treated, in Ribicoff's words, like the "national scold."

9

All That Money

APPEARING BEFORE A SENATE COMMITTEE IN NOVEMBER 1971, Ralph Nader said indignantly, "We know more about the CIA than is known about the internal workings of GM." He was singing, as the *New York Times* deferentially noted, an old song. "Mr. Nader proposed a number of recommendations," it reported, "on corporate secrecy practices to the committee. Some of the proposals had been presented before by Mr. Nader, such as making corporate income tax returns public and increasing disclosure of corporate activities."

The irony of his indignation, however, did not reach Nader. General Motors was a private company, doing business for profit and not asking the public for contributions and making public disclosure of all information required by law in its financial reports to stockholders. Nader, on the other hand, was soliciting funds from individuals and foundations for his activities. But how much he got and from whom—and how he spent it—was information he shared with no one but the Internal Revenue Service. All attempts by friendly reporters to get some kind of accounting from Nader of his public trust were airily or angrily brushed aside. Finally, he reluctantly promised that he would tell all by the summer of 1973. It was, he said, very complicated.

But summer gave way to fall, fall to winter, and winter to the spring of 1974, and Nader still remained silent. Like the CIA, the financial side of Ralph Nader remained shrouded in dark secrecy —and those with a legitimate curiosity about the millions he had taken in and, presumably, the millions he had spent, never received any satisfaction. Complicated or not, Nader continued to collect and disburse without opening his books to those who had given him one dollar or one hundred thousand dollars. The more charitable suggested that a man who operated as haphazardly as Nader probably did not know. This, of course, raised a few eyebrows. But the Washington press corps, which by its bulldog tenacity compelled full disclosure of President Nixon's finances, somehow showed little interest in getting Nader to do likewise.

There were, however, some puzzling aspects about the Nader finances. After paying his lawyers, he had been left with $280,000 in the settlement of his suit for invasion of privacy against General Motors—all tax-free. But this, by his own statement, had been contributed *in toto* to his Public Interest Research Group. In subsequent reports, however, it developed that he had turned over $170,000 a year for two years to the PIRG out of his General Motors money—or $340,000, which would have been a neat bit of bookkeeping. And when he mounted his half-million dollar Congress Project, he again let it be known that the funds would come from the GM settlement, making it the most elastic sum of money since the days of the Grant administration.

It may have been that these reports were the result of careless talk by his subordinates, picked up by the press, and published without checking. However, Nader had also informed biographer McCarry that he intended to support PIRG with the money he received from his highly profitable lecture appearances. But Nader also sent two PIRG aides, Donald Ross and James Welch, to beat the hinterland bushes for contributions, and these came to well over a million dollars.

Late in 1971, Nader created Public Citizen, Inc., soliciting supporters to contribute $15 each, hoping to establish a mass base for his operations. Some 62,000 people responded, sending anywhere from a dollar to five thousand for a total of $1.1 million, to the full-page newspaper advertisements and the direct mail campaign for funds. At the time Public Citizen was announced, the *Washington Daily News* reported, "An accounting of how much money comes in . . . and how it is spent is not promised."

The trail of contributions to the Nader crusade, however, begins with the Center for the Study of Responsive Law, from which a baker's dozen of other Nader organizations sprang more or less fully armed. The Center was, and is, tax-exempt—though a suspicious mind might conceive that it has stretched past the breaking point any contention that it is not in the business of influencing public policy and lobbying for legislation—both of which could justify the lifting of that exemption by a less-tolerant Internal Revenue Service. In mid-1970, an inquisitive columnist* decided that it might be of interest to his readers to learn just how much money the Center was taking in, how much it was spending.

Since tax-exempt organizations must file an information return, Form 990, which is open to public examination, the columnist dispatched a researcher to the Washington IRS office to get a copy of the 1969 return. Though it was a month past the filing date, the researcher was informed in writing that IRS had "no record" of any return. On seven occasions, up to September 9, 1970, the researcher applied for a copy of the Center's return and was told that there was "no record"—all of this in writing. At this point, the columnist sat down at his typewriter to produce the following, after having made several fruitless attempts to reach the Center's executive director, Theodore Jacobs:

HOW RESPONSIVE TO THE LAW IS NADER?

Ralph Nader, man for all seasons of the "consumer" movement, may find himself unseasonable on one count: He failed to file a return with the Internal Revenue Service for the Center for the Study of Responsive Law, which he heads. The Center is tax-exempt but must file Form 990-A annually if it is to retain that exemption. According to IRS, which made a search for the Center's 1969 return, it cannot be found.

Mr. Nader, who lectures the business community and the Federal government on ethics and responsiveness to law, is a hard man to reach, but he will have some difficulty explaining one other troublesome fact. Gary Sellers, an aide to Representative Philip Burton (D.-Cal.), lists as his office address 1908 Q Street, N.W., and as his office telephone 462-8800—the address and phone number of the Center. A call to Congressman Burton's office elicited the information that Mr. Sellers was not around "but might well be at the Q Street address."

No plea of ignorance can account for Mr. Nader's failure to file . . . In 1968, when the Center's income was $4,500, Mr. Nader properly filed a return. In 1969, when the Center's income was reportedly $95,000 [in fact, it was $173,117], the return was ignored. Strangely enough, IRS, which has been asked some questions about Mr. Nader's lack of compliance, has done nothing to determine the why and wherefore.

There is no mystery about where most of the $95,000 contributed to the Center for the Study of Responsive Law came from. The

*Not to be coy about it, Ralph de Toledano.

96

Carnegie Corporation of New York, which then listed among its trustees *New York Times* executive vice president Harding Bancroft, turned over $55,000 to the Center. Two other foundations—the New York Foundation, among whose trustees were members of the Sulzberger family, owners of the *New York Times*, and the New World Foundation, whose board of directors included *New York Times* London Bureau chief Anthony Lewis—contributed another $10,000 each.

This interlocking support may answer some questions about the tremendous backing that Mr. Nader and the Center have received from certain elements of the press. But of far more interest is the fact that Form 990-A asks pointedly: "During the year, did you . . . advocate or oppose any national, state, or local legislation?" Mr. Nader's lobbying activities are well known to any reader of the daily prints. His close relationship—and that of the Center—with a man on the congressional payroll assumes some significance in this context.*

. . . . Of . . . value to the Center was Mr. Sellers, one of the architects of the Coal Mine Safety Act—a measure for which Mr. Nader lobbied intensively. It should be noted here that this bill came up before the House Education and Labor Committee, of which Mr. Sellers' congressional employer is a member . . . As kingpin in the Center for the Study of Responsive Law, he is now demonstrating his own responsiveness to the nation's legal structure.

Two days after the column had been written and mailed to the syndicate which then distributed it, still another check was made at IRS, at which time a copy of the column was shown to a member of the staff, who found it accurate and once again said there was "no record of filing." Three hours later, by one of those thundering "coincidences" which make Washington reporting such an adventure, IRS phoned to say that it had located the Center's return but that it was not available. It took four days—and a threat by the researcher that he would not move out of the IRS office until he was given a copy—before the columnist was able to examine what purported to be the Center's 1969 return. It was a curious-looking document, handwritten, with no employer number and with entries crossed out as if it were a rough draft. Most curious of all, it did not have the date stamp which is routinely applied by IRS on all returns when they are received.

Nader's reply to the column was typical: a telegram to such

*When the return was finally produced, the question was answered by a "No."

newspapers as he thought had published it accusing the columnist of "falsehoods and misrepresentations" and claiming that he had "admitted to the Center's executive director, Theodore J. Jacobs, that he learned a few hours after he wrote the column that the return had in fact been filed"—an accusation cut from the whole cloth. Nader also "answered" a number of points never mentioned in the column and demonstrated his sense of the moral and accurate by stating, in regard to Gary Sellers, that he was "a part-time consultant to the Center"—though not mentioning that Sellers had received $10,100 for his labors. "What else he does to advise a member of Congress who requests his technical help has no connection with the Center," Nader said, ignoring the fact that Sellers was on a congressional staff and therefore violating the House's Code of Ethics.

In 1971, efforts to obtain the Center's Form 990 again were arduous, but they did turn up one interesting fact. The Center had filed one return, filed an "amended return," and then filed an identical amended return. Of this IRS wrote: "It is not known why the same amended return was filed on two separate dates." The 1970 return disclosed that the Center had received $380,406 in gifts and grants from a long list of tax-exempt foundations and individuals, including Mr. and Mrs. Martin Peretz, consistent patrons of New Left causes. The largest contribution, $100,000, came from the Midas International Corporation Foundation—the first part of a promised $300,000—and there is no record that Nader felt any compuction about taking money from the manufacturer of an automobile part. There was also a $5,000 contribution from the Public Safety Research Institute, which had been established by Nader with a $150,000 gift from a sympathetic multimillionaire, Robert Townsend. On June 9, 1973, *National Journal*, an offshoot of the prestigious *Congressional Quarterly*, reported:

> During 1973, Public Citizen is financing the total budget of six Nader organizations and parts of the budgets of four others.
> Those fully financed are Public Citizen Litigation Group ($75,000); Citizen Action Group ($50,000); Tax Reform Research Group ($125,000); Retired Professional Action Group ($45,000); Health Research Group ($110,000); and Congress Watch ($100,000).
> Other groups that received Public Citizen funds in 1972 are the Aviation Consumer Action Group ($8,000); the Small Claims Study Group ($9,500); the Institute for Women's Policy Studies ($10,000); Professional Drivers Council for Health and Safety ($4,000); and one

grassroots organization, the Connecticut Citizens' Action Group ($25,000).

This comes to $561,500. Of the $1.1 million collected by Public Citizen, Inc., the organization netted some $800,000, according to a timid Nader aide who asked not to be identified, the balance going to the costs in direct mail and advertising. Nader has said that he makes somewhere between $150,000 and $175,000, though some have set the figure at $500,000. He has also said that he spends some $5,000 a year on himself, a somewhat deceptive figure since he spends much of the year traveling, during which time his living expenses are paid by those who have engaged his services. This income, according to Nader, comes from "two sources—lecturing and writing, mostly writing." But a search of Library of Congress files indicates that much of Nader's writing output is letters to the editor, which pay nothing, introductions to books, which pay little, and articles for small publications, which pay even less. For his lectures, however, he charges between $2,500 and $3,500. According to biographer Buckhorn, he will deliver as many as eight lectures a day when he is on the road.

Where does all this money go—this income that far exceeds what most corporate executives make? Since IRS has not yet bowed to Nader's demands for an end to tax secrecy—and since he has steadfastly avoided publication of his own returns—the only answer to be found is in Nader's own statements. He has repeatedly said that he plows back all of his income into the consumer movement, with the exception of the little he uses to satisfy the landlord of his twenty-dollar-a-week room, to pay for the aggressively ill-fitting suits he wears, or to purchase the "unadulterated" foods that keep body and soul together.

Nader, however, told *National Journal* that he had personally financed the Congress Project and the Public Interest Research Group—not mentioning that he had collected more than a million from contributions to the PIRG. This, he said, left him "tremendously in the hole in 1972"—to the tune of "close to $300,000." Where that $300,000 came from, since there has been no hint that Nader borrowed it from the bank, deponent sayeth not. It may be another thundering coincidence, but the difference between what Public Citizen netted and what it spent is roughly $300,000.

Under ordinary circumstances, this shuffling of funds—if such it is—from Nader front to Nader transmission belt—would be of no consequence. But Public Citizen, Inc., is tax-exempt. Its monies cannot be used for lobbying or influencing public policy, which is Ralph Nader's main activity, when he is not carrying his message to the heathen. But the questions raised cannot be answered until Nader lets those who support him and his causes know where he gets his money, how he gets it, and how he spends it. Interestingly, those who have sought to make some fiscal sense of his finances always forget one fact. If he earns $200,000, he can spend only a half of that on his causes—unless the Internal Revenue Service has waived the tax statute or made history by declaring his person a tax-exempt institution.

10

Nader as Legislator

TO THOSE WHO COMPLAIN THAT RALPH NADER'S FACTS TEND TO be fictional and his figures fanciful, the standard answer has been that true though this may be, he is responsible for a great deal of important and necessary legislation which has saved lives and curbed the rapaciousness of American business. If this were true, then Nader's tantrums, his wholesale slaughter of innocents, and the reputations he has left lying by the wayside might almost be worth it. But even the most cursory examination of the legislation for which Nader claims credit could document the charge that it has done more harm than good. Writing in the *Washington Post,* a newspaper in the forefront of Nader adulators, William Greider made the point clearly:

> Let's suppose, just to be mischievous, that some public-spirited citizen appointed a "task force" to investigate Ralph Nader.
>
> Following Nader's example, he probably would recruit a dozen or so college students, very bright and self-confident, to spend their summer poring over what Nader has done for the American consumer. After months of legwork, they call a press conference and issue their massive report, couched in language which is appropriately inflammatory:
>
> "The purity of Ralph Nader's outrage is exceeded only by the ineffectiveness of his solutions . . . Like the auto makers who design cosmetic tailfins, Nader has added more remnant parts for the already cluttered governmental machinery. Thanks to Nader, consumers pay higher prices; their tax dollars support more bureaucrats. The results are mixed at best and, in some cases, have actually

resulted in extra protection for the producers, not the consumers whom Nader supposedly represents.

"There is more truth than fancy in this make-believe scenario," Greider concluded, adding that the "concrete contributions" made by Nader in the field of legislation "fall far short of what Nader might call a victory." Not noted by Greider, though, and one of the signal results of Nader activities on Capitol Hill, has been his success in antagonizing hitherto enthusiastic "consumerists" in House and Senate and planting deep suspicions in their minds of Nader's cause.

In the field of car safety, Nader had taken the focus of public concern off the major cause of accidents—the drinking driver. Legislation and government pressure began the process of removing lead from gasoline before there was any valid proof that this increased air pollution or caused any damage to the human body. It did, however, decrease mileage per gallon at a time of fuel shortages and increased the consumer's bill. Other safety measures, like the seat belt, were being ignored by a preponderance of riders, but they had increased the cost of cars. The loss to the economy was incalculable, and to respect for law equally so.

Nader and his agents in the Congress had pushed through a mine safety law which was to protect miners—and Nader made much of this in his speeches and fund-raising efforts. But deaths in the mines, under Nader's "safety" law, had increased from 203 in 1969 to 260 in 1970—and injuries had also risen. The only triumph was one of rhetoric.

Nader had also made much of his effectiveness in getting Congress to pass a gas pipeline safety law. But more than two years later, the *Washington Post* was able to report that it was a "leaky piece of legislation" whose net effect had been "to lower safety standards . . . Meanwhile the fatalities from gas pipeline explosions have been increasing for the past two years." Nader himself, in moments of candor, calls the legislation he sired "an utter failure," though he has not bothered to put his finger on where the blame lies—namely that the law he argued for simply deprived the states of their regulatory powers and dumped them on a federal bureaucracy which cannot cope. Had Nader known anything about the pipeline industry—and had he been equipped with more than hatred and strong language—he would have been less ready to shoot from the hip. Said the *Washington Post*, "Several states like New York are complaining that the new federal standards have actually lowered their level of safety enforcement."

Nader basked in the approval that came his way when, as a result of his outcries, Congress passed a meat inspection law which extended to intrastate packing houses the purity standards demanded by the federal government. There has been no improvement in the sanitary conditions of packing plants—in fact, the contrary. And the consequences of Nader's reforms may well be the destruction of the regulatory system set up many decades ago as a result of the efforts by Upton Sinclair and the early muckrakers. Nader, of course, found others to blame—Congress, the executive branch, and the public, all three too lazy or too corrupt to stand up to the "special interests" he finds lurking around every corner.

Nader's failure as a part-time legislator derives from his *modus operandi* and from the sheer intolerance of his approach. On the one hand, he has always believed that a handful of college students can go through a regulatory agency or a complex problem and come up with easy answers which can be embodied in a simplistic piece of legislation. On the other hand, he isolates himself from the realities of life by seeing the mark of Cain on all men. "The trouble with working with Ralph," one liberal lobbyist told the press, "is that Ralph insists he is the only honest man in the world." The net effect of this is a dwindling of his support as one earnest consumerist after another is denounced by Nader because he has not brought Heaven to earth overnight. His methodology is best exemplified in his relations with Representative Chet Holifield and in the battle to create a consumer department in the cabinet.

On October 13, 1972, Holifield took the floor of the House to inform the members of what Ralph had wrought. Said the California Democrat, a card-carrying liberal and dedicated consumerist:

> The 92nd Congress is about to adjourn without passing the bill to establish an independent Consumer Protection Agency . . . Why did the consumer legislation fail? . . . The consumer bill was killed by some of its avowed friends as well as its enemies. Take Ralph Nader, who is reputed to be the great friend of the consumer. By insisting on the politically impossible, he helped get us nothing at all . . .
>
> How did this come about? The crucial time was one year ago. Remember that the consumer bill passed the House . . . by an overwhelming vote of 344 to 44. A Senate subcommittee held hearings shortly thereafter, and Mr. Nader was a key witness.

What did this self-appointed consumers' advocate do? He urged the Senate subcommittee to lay the bill aside until the following year. This was done. The momentum of the House action was lost . . . Why did Mr. Nader press for delay? Well, he fancied himself a political expert, and the bill which we passed in the House did not suit him . . .

I do not want to exaggerate Mr. Nader's importance in influencing legislation, but neither do I want to underrate it. He had the greatest reputation in the country as the consumers' friend, and he misused that friendship. He became obsessed with maintaining his prestige rather than seeking practical means of getting legislation through the Congress.

The story of Mr. Nader's role in the failure of the consumer legislation bears telling in some detail, Mr. Speaker, because it is not well understood. There has been much error and confusion in the press coverage of this complicated affair. Also, some deliberate falsehoods have been bandied about by Mr. Nader and his partisans . . .

The story had begun when Nader and a group of congressmen, the so-called Nader group in the House which scratches whenever the "people's lawyer" itches, attempted to develop legislation for an independent consumer agency. In December 1970, the House Committee on Government Operations reported out a consumer bill which had Nader's imprimatur and had been largely drafted by his volunteers. But it was, as even those most dedicated to consumerism admitted, badly written. Not only were too many conflicting ideas imbedded in its text, but it did not bother to define "consumer" or "consumer interests"—making it legally vulnerable. And it had, as Holifield conceded, "excessively broad powers of investigation" among other controversial features. After careful study, the House Rules Committee killed the bill, setting forth a long list of objections which consumerists recognized. In the 92nd Congress, a Holifield subcommittee held extensive hearings and came up with H.R. 10835—a bill which included much of the old bill as well as the needed definitions and safeguards.

This time the Rules Committee let it go through [Holifield told the House]. Although not all its members were supporters of the consumer bill . . . they recognized that we had done a workmanlike job and that the bill made more sense than before . . .

The approach from the left, led by the Nader group, would have made the Consumer Protection Agency a super agency with unnecessary snooping powers . . . a mean, nasty fellow with brass knuckles . . . Yielding to the Nader group would have meant defeat in the House of Representatives . . .

The House of Representatives chose to walk a middle path on consumer legislation. It passed a strong and effective bill . . . This middle path made sense politically because it was the best bill we could get. It also made sense administratively . . . The overwhelming vote in the House of 344 to 44 vindicated our position on the consumer bill.

But Ralph Nader was furious that the House of Representatives did not bow to his judgment or to his demands. As usual, he ascribed this failure to understand his real worth to deliberate malice and/or corruption. And as the "only honest man in the world," he saw in the defeat of his totalitarian measure a sellout by Holifield and others in the Congress to Big Business. Holifield, he charged, was a tool of the White House who had deliberately sabotaged a good bill because President Nixon had given him a ride on the presidential plane. Holifield had been flown only once in Air Force One, months before the consumer bill was under consideration. Nader therefore invented a second trip, dutifully reported by the Nader press, in which the president had persuaded Holifield to support "an administration version of a consumer-protection law."

This fiction was nourished by a Nader henchman and would-be lobbyist, one Gary Sellers [Holifield reported]. He spread the false rumor that I was peddling a "secret draft" of a consumer bill, prepared by White House aides, and he tried to persuade a Los Angeles representative of the Consumer Federation of America to organize a picket line in front of my district office in Pico River, California. Failing in this, he arranged a picket line of his own. The pickets carried signs protesting this (wholly imaginary) "secret draft."

In the course of the hearings, the Holifield subcommittee heard testimony from friends and foes of the consumer protection bill. It would have been remiss in its duties had it only asked for the views of those who favored it, as Nader would have preferred. Among those called to testify was Roger C. Crampton, chairman of the Administrative Conference of the United States, a body of experts under congressional oversight whose mission it is to study and recommend improvements in federal administration. Nader and his press friends made it appear that Crampton was a White House official, sent to Congress to oppose a consumer agency. And fed by the Nader publicity machine, newspapers misrepresented the provisions of the Holifield bill to prove that it was a conspiratorial attempt by the White House and the special interests to saddle the country with evil legislation.

> Many fictions were spread by Mr. Nader and his aides . . . One of their more vivid fantasies was that the gentlemen from Arkansas, Mr. [Wilbur] Mills, the distinguished chairman of the Committee on Ways and Means, was in the Nader camp . . . When this proved to be fantasy and not fact, Mr. Nader made insulting remarks about Chairman Mills.
>
> In Mr. Nader's eyes the difference between a hero and a villain is whether or not one agrees with him . . . If he does not play the Nader game, he is public enemy No. 1.
>
> . . . Mr. Nader referred to the bill as a "legislative fraud against the consumers." He charged me with gutting the bill. He announced to the press: "Chairman Holifield, the White House, and the business lobby have won today."

Having failed to impose his will on the House, Nader moved over to the Senate—but with a difference. Before a Senate committee holding hearings on H.R. 10835, he argued strenuously against any bill. The following year would be an election year, he told the senators. Pressure on House members from their constituents would compel them to write the kind of bill he wanted. But wouldn't Senate inaction seriously slow the momentum for consumer legislation? Senator Charles Percy, a liberal Republican with strong consumerist views, put the question to Nader. "No," Nader answered flatly. In an election year, moreover, the Senate would have greater clout as it bargained for a stronger bill in conference. And then, out of his long inexperience, he attempted to drive a wedge between House and Senate.

"Have you ever talked to the senior members of the House of Representatives about how they view the senators' role in a conference committee?" he asked Senator Percy. "To describe their attitude as utter contempt and overconfidence would be an understatement."

The Senate Government Operations subcommittee considering consumer legislation accepted the advice of the country's greatest consumerist. It was almost a year before the parent committee reported out its own version of the House bill, incorporating some of Nader's provisions. But, as Holifield had predicted, the momentum was lost and the bill was killed by a filibuster. And during this period, when help from Nader was needed the most, he was busy with other matters. As Holifield reported to his colleagues:

> Through all the filibustering on the Senate side, nothing much was heard publicly from Mr. Nader until he dashed off a telegram to a one-time Nader Raider, Mr. Edward Cox, son-in-law of President Nixon . . . Mr. Nader urged Mr. Cox to appeal to the President to save the consumer bill . . .

The telegram to Cox was a grandstand play, indicating Nader's total lack of understanding of government and the legislative process. To begin with, his intervention came too late. Secondly, it presupposed that President Nixon would overrule his advisers in favor of counsel from his son-in-law. And most important of all, it irritated some of the senators who wanted no secondhand intervention. Had Nader been willing to put in the time and effort to work with consumerist senators and to mobilize public opinion, a consumer agency bill would have been enacted. But that is not Ralph Nader's way.

> There is irony in all this [Holifield told the House], and also an object lesson. Mr. Nader, who claims to be the consumers' friend, has been instrumental in denying to consumers an effective government agency for their protection . . .
> There are those who say that Mr. Nader wanted an issue instead of a bill. They hazard the belief that this self-styled and self-appointed consumer advocate wants to be a one-man Consumer Protection Agency; that he is afraid that once the agency is created by law, the steam will go out of his own enterprise and the sources of his financial support will dry up.
> Perhaps so, Mr. Speaker, but I would prefer to identify a more serious issue . . . Mr. Nader was not interested in the politics of constructive achievement. Yes, he played politics of constructive achievement. Yes, he played politics, but it was his own brand of politics . . . He wanted to rule or ruin. In the case of the consumer bill, saving face was more important for him than saving the legislation . . .
> Taking on the whole Congress seems absurd to many but not to Mr. Nader. He is corrupted by the illusion of power. He seems to think that being on the right side of causes automatically endows him with superior wisdom . . . He was trapped by his own ambitions and the numerous misconceptions he spread about. His opposition

to our bill was marked by increasing stridency and exaggeration. Never once did he state fairly the provisions of the House bill. Now the legislative program for consumer protection lies in shambles.

This, of course, was not the way Nader's waterboys in the media reported it. He was given high marks for his principled approach. And he was encouraged in the belief that he and his movement could twist the arm of Congress into doing exactly as he wanted. The result of this miscalculation was the Congress Project, which cost him, by his own admission, "about half a million dollars" from sources unknown.

The purpose of the project was to "expose" the shortcomings of Congress—or so it was stated. But behind it was Nader's desire to punish the Congress for not allowing him to order its procedures and dictate the kind of legislation he demanded. The Congress Project,* however, exposed the Nader methodology to senators and representatives who had known of the man and his movement only through the public prints. It guaranteed that Nader's effectiveness as a consumer lobbyist would sharply decline—and that the wild pronouncements which once impressed the Congress would be subjected to sharp and careful scrutiny.

*See Chapter 8.

108

11

The Environmentalist
Frolic

RALPH NADER HAD MADE HIS MARK ON THE PUBLIC CONSCIOUS-
ness as the man who slew the Corvair and humbled General Motors. From there, he had risen to the role of consumer advocate.
But it was mandatory for him, if he was to survive, to move from
field to field, like a guerrilla fighter striking and running before the
opposition could unlimber its guns. His mail, moreover, disclosed
that much of the public thought of him as a glorified toaster repair-
man. If a gadget did not work, the purchaser could write his
complaint to Ralph Nader.

There was logic, then, in Nader's shift to the productive and
lucrative environmentalist trade. His sorties against the automobile had resulted in the successful enactment by Congress of some
"safety" regulations, one of which would presumably reduce air
pollution in the nation's cities and towns, and for this he had been
widely hailed by the environmentalist claque which ignored the
lamentations of the auto industry and of many car owners. As in
most of what Nader achieved, more harm than good was done—
and even the usually reverential *New York Times* belatedly noted
that the devices touted by Nader to cut down on auto emissions
"could create a bigger medical risk than the ones they were designed to remove."

Scientists, still unheard by the environmentalists and by Congress, were pointing out that the exhaust-cleaning mechanisms
being installed in new cars, at a cost of billions to the consumer,
might well kill more people than they saved. These mechanisms
employed platinum and palladium to convert noxious hydrocar-
bons and carbon monoxide in car exhausts into harmless carbon

dioxide and water. But they also converted even microscopic traces of sulfur in gasoline into sulfuric acid mists and other deadly substances. "The sulfate residue," said the *New York Times* in reporting the concern of scientists, "could build up to dangerous levels on freeways or city streets in stagnant air situations which often occur in Los Angeles and occasionally in East Coast cities."

This did not particularly trouble Nader, since his knowledge of science is secondary to his capabilities as a propagandist. As an environmentalist, he simply picked up what others had charged, and without the bother of intensive investigation repeated the charge more emphatically. In an interview which ran to twelve columns in *National Wildlife* magazine, Nader ranged the field in a manner which, quoting Pope, would "amaze the unlearned and make the learned smile":

> I think there are going to be serious genetic consequences and serious health consequences in this country if we fail within the next twenty years to make contamination of the environment a crime, a crime with serious penalties . . . A million pounds of mercury are thrown into the waterways and yet until recently we didn't know that mercury decomposes into the kind of subconstituents that go into the fish. The same is true of oil . . . Oil breaks down into carcinogenic elements that are then consumed by fish. The devastating effect of oil spills are being uncovered with increasing frequency all the time [*sic*].

Nader was simply parroting what he had heard during the mercury-in-fish scare—or hoax—of 1970–71, when environmentalists were claiming that the mercury content in fish has increased "fifty to one hundred times" as a result of the rising industrial use of that metal and the outpouring of waste from plants employing it. He either did not know or suppressed the outcome of the great national scare. By analyzing fossils, fish preserved by the Smithsonian Institution, and so forth, scientists discovered that the amount of mercury in fish had remained constant for the past two thousand years. They also discovered that there was frequently a larger amount of mercury in fish living in waters untouched by industrial waste than in those which had been exposed to mercury-tainted industrial effluents.

Nader's science-fiction about oil spills could have only been the result of irresponsible ignorance or suppression of the facts. There had been a great to-do about the Santa Barbara Channel oil spill, thoroughly orchestrated by the environmentalists who had screamed of "hundreds of thousands" of dead fish and of a permanently destroyed waterway, ecologically speaking. The facts, duly publicized after the environmentalist uproar, was that the Santa Barbara type of oil rig blowout was a rarity. Of the 1,500 offshore wells operated by Standard Oil, only three had ever blown out— with very small effect. The "hundreds of thousands" of fish killed turned out to be four thousand. Within months, more fish had been caught in the channel than before the accident. Of far greater significance was the discovered fact that more oil seeps into the oceans through natural fissures than all the oil spilled as a result of drilling. In fact, moreover, pumping oil from offshore wells reduces the pressure and lessens the amount of natural seepage. If fish are carcinogenic today, they were carcinogenic thousands of years ago, before the hated oil companies existed. Nader's assertions were therefore childish gobbledegook.

Motivated by his desire to throttle industry, Nader cries, "Stop the world!" but he won't get off. For this, he must have much on his conscience. Speaking in Houston on October 29, 1971, he denounced the first warnings of the Nixon administration and the oil industry of an impending energy crisis as profiteering lies. Both the administration and the industry were "making false claims" of imminent shortages to frighten the consumer into paying higher prices for gasoline, Nader said. "They're finding oil faster than the public can consume it," he charged. "They have developed enormous oil reserves and equally enormous restrictions which keep prices up." And the oil companies were also guilty of air pollution.

Five months before this Nader speech, President Nixon had attempted to rouse Congress and the public from their apathy and to prod the country into seeking new sources of energy to meet sharply accelerating energy demands. Nader's outburst encouraged a public complacency which contributed to the crisis when his fellow Arabs hit the world with an oil embargo after the Yom Kippur war in the Middle East and sent prices skyrocketing.

By September 1973, however, Nader had shrewdly withdrawn his picture of a United States swimming in surplus oil. He continued to hold up the oil industry as a culprit, however, orating that it had been "calculatingly developing a short-term energy crisis in order to get what it wants out of Washington." The American Petroleum Institute answered sharply that if Nader had any evidence of this, it was his duty to present it to a grand jury. "If he has no proof, he is doing the public a disservice by adding to the confusion surrounding the energy issue," the API said. But Nader's charges were carried by network television, whereas the API rebuttal was issued as a news release which much of the media ignored.

Equally ignored—or scoffed at—were the words of Frank N. Ikard, head of the API. "Both gasoline and distillate production," he pointed out, "set all-time records during the first five months of 1973." The shortages were the result of an "unprecedented growth in demand" and the opposition from Nader and the environmentalists who marched under his banner to all means of meeting that demand. Said Ikard:

> Restrictions have been placed on the mining and the use of coal ... Shortages of natural gas have been created by its environmental advantages ... On the gasoline side, a major factor is the loss of miles per gallon in the newer automobiles equipped with pollution control devices These controls have been estimated to increase gasoline consumption by 12.6 million gallons a day.

Environmentalist sabotage and unwarranted concern over the mating habits of the caribou had blocked the development of Alaska's North Slope oil. Wells in the Santa Barbara Channel had been capped. And because of pressure from the environmentalists, the use of cleaner-burning oil, instead of coal, in the production of electricity had risen from eight thousand barrels a day in 1967 to two hundred thousand barrels a day in 1973. Congress, moreover, had set up regulations for the removal of sulfur from coal, basing them on a nonexistent technology—the work of Nader and his friends.

By mid-December, Nader had taken cognizance of the country's unhappiness and had shifted back to his old position that, Arab embargo or no Arab embargo, the energy shortage was "the most phony [*sic*] crisis ever inflicted upon a modern society." (Clearly, there was no shortage of hyperbole.) The country was still swimming in oil, he argued, but the oil companies were hiding vast stores from the public. As the "people's lawyer" he might have been expected to provide evidence of this, but he merely referred to unsubstantiated rumors, offering them as fact. He compromised his case by adding that there would be no shortages if industry did not "waste" fuel—and he called for the kind of mandatory and government-imposed cutbacks on oil usage by industry

112

which would have put millions of workers on the unemployment rolls.

But where Nader, as boy environmentalist, made his real push was in the nuclear energy field—and here again, his "solutions" spelled tragedy for the nation and for all of its consumers. Basing his opposition to nuclear power on little more than bile and prejudice, he was advising that it must be rejected out of hand. No matter that some parts of the country were already dependent on nuclear power or that projections showed that it could supply most electrical energy needs by the year 2000.* Nader argued: "If the country knew what the facts were and if they had to choose between nuclear reactors and candles, they would choose candles."

To force this country to accept his scientifically illiterate ideas, Nader joined forces with Friends of the Earth, one of the interlocked groups of extremist eco-freaks, in a suit filed with a Federal court in Washington to compel the Atomic Energy Commission to withdraw the operating licenses of twenty nuclear power plants. In this suit, he was being advised by the Union of Concerned Scientists, a tiny activist organization discredited by 99 percent of the scientific community. Ironically, had Nader succeeded in this effort, the country would have been compelled to return to the extensive use of the coal which Nader insisted was contributing vastly to air pollution. As Consumers Power of Michigan, operator of the Palisades nuclear plant, one of those Nader hoped to shut down, stated, theirs was

the most efficient, lowest-fuel-cost, base-load plant on [our] entire system. If this plant were shut down, the loss of generating capacity would have to be made up by older, less efficient fossil plants burning coal and oil, thus adding to adverse environmental effects. Moreover, with the loss of Palisades, Consumers Power would have to purchase additional capacity from its neighboring utilities, with the prospect of the availability of such purchase extremely dim. The added cost, on top of the environmental effects would be staggering. Palisades, in a year, would generate 5 billion kilowatt hours. The cost of generating this same 5 billion kilowatt hours, either with Consumers' generating plants or a neighboring utility's plants using

*In Illinois, Commonwealth Edison's use of uranium fuel was substituting in 1974 for 12 million tons of coal or 41 million barrels of oil.

older, less efficient units, could run five times the Palisades costs, or nearly $40 million difference annually.

Obviously, Nader the ecologist was in conflict with Nader the consumer advocate since the added costs would be passed down to the purchasers. If Nader had been able to sustain his shrilly argued contention that nuclear power was a threat to the life and health of Americans, then it would be obvious where his duty lay. But did nuclear power plants pose a real threat? Or was Nader broadcasting unwarranted fears to justify his passion for slowing down the economy? Were facts and figures being distorted or invented to prove his point?*

Like Nader's other campaigns, the appeal was not to reason and was marked by *ad hominem* attacks on those who disagreed with him, plus uncontrolled hyperbole. Of Dixy Lee Ray, who chaired the Atomic Energy Commission, Nader said that "she is suffering from professional insanity" and that she was "locked into a bureaucratic momentum that has so distorted her capacity for reason that she is leading the Atomic Energy into this drive for technological suicide, through nuclear fission." Recalling the frenzy of those "scientists" who in the early fifties predicted that the Eniwetok tests would split the earth in half and set the atmosphere ablaze, Nader accused the Joint Congressional Committee on Atomic Energy, one of the most responsible in the Congress, of deliberately suppressing the "great hazards of nuclear power." In abusive language, he told off its members and demanded that they shut down nuclear power plants because "the risks of accident and sabotage are at a point of catastrophic consequence unparalleled in the history of mankind."

Nader demanded this shutdown of all nuclear plants unless the committee and the AEC could guarantee an absolutely accident-free performance—criteria which if applied to airplanes, the automobile, or the bathtub would ban them all. In a rebuttal of Nader, Dr. Ralph Lapp, a member of the energy policy committee of the militantly ecological Sierra Club, wrote in the *New York Times Magazine* that "the risk of being bitten by a rattlesnake in

*Other environmentalists were doing precisely that. In the December 15, 1970, *Look*, an article by Jack Shepherd, in warning against nuclear power, stated that fourteen workers had died of cancer at the Rocky Cliffs nuclear plant. What Shepherd failed to note was that the fourteen cancer deaths, in relation to the number of people employed at the plant, were *below* the national average. The "statistic" was true but meaningless—and deliberately intended to frighten the public.

114

Times Square is low, but not zero. The chance of being hit by a car is fairly high. People accept the risk of death involved in traveling on a common carrier, such as an airline—that risk is about one in a million for each flight"—exactly the figure Dixy Lee Ray had used as the possibility of a serious, nuclear-related accident in a nuclear plant.

For the most part, Nader's attack on the development of nuclear power consisted of little more than fright-wig generalities. Had he been tested on his real knowledge of nuclear science, he would have been hard pressed to explain the substance of a 22,000-page, eighteen-month study of the uses and risks of nuclear energy, prepared by the AEC. And he would have backed away from statements in that report, whose meaning he did not know, such as: "The time to DNB is computed using the W-3 critical heat flux correlation in both the CRAFT and THETA 1-B codes, except that the B&W-2 correlation is used in THETA 1-B for the nonvent plants."

To make his point, Nader added up all the nonnuclear accidents and malfunctions of nuclear plants and presented them as if they were all nuclear-related. He stated falsely that nuclear plants were unsafe and untried by citing accidents and breakdowns in their nonnuclear activity—and never once noted that breakdowns and shutdowns of nuclear plants were numerically far less than those of conventional plants. That no member of the public had ever been hurt in the operation of any nuclear power plant was of no concern to him. Neither was the AEC's record of only seven radiation-associated deaths in more than thirty years—a record which included the early days of nuclear experimentation and a crash weapons program. He railed against the nuclear wastes of commercial plants, which are minor, lumping them with those of weapons plants which produce the preponderance of such wastes.

The Nader methodology was best demonstrated in an article for general newspaper distribution. He noted first that President Nixon had "reassuringly" asserted that his San Clemente property was only a few miles away from a nuclear power facility. "What he didn't tell [the press]," Nader said ominously, "is that this plant at San Onofre, California, had closed down for several months on October 21 [1973] due to a serious and costly accident." What Nader did not tell his readers was that this accident had no connection with the nuclear components of the plant. The accident had been to a turbine blade in an electric generator.

The Nader article further warned of "a catastrophic chain reaction" which in some malfunctions "would release radioactivity into the environment." This, as one veteran nuclear engineer pointed out, "borders on complete falsehood." Anyone at all familiar with the design of commercial nuclear reactors knew, the engineer stated, that such a chain reaction was impossible in commercial reactor plants. In the "remote chance" of a meltdown of the nuclear core, what Nader was talking about, "the radioactivity would be contained by a thick-walled containment vessel specially designed for this purpose."

In listing nuclear plant hazards, Nader wrote that "another recently discovered defect affects certain reactors manufactured by General Electric and the adequacy of reactor cooling." Morris Hulin, a nuclear engineer, rebutted this with: "Again condemnation by accusation without supporting facts. If he is referring to the recent de-rating of GE fuel, that was a warranty measure, and was not related to safety but to economics." Nader also made noises about the ECCS, the emergency core cooling system which eliminates the possible hazard of a meltdown, which he described as "deficient" and of "varying reliability," basing his criticism on no known evidence but on his ignorance of the subject and his own dark fears. ECCS has, when called into use, always been successful and is strongly defended by nuclear scientists and engineers.

Naturally Nader had his "secret" document, presumably turned over to him by one of his spies at the AEC. This document, Nader said, had been "suppressed" because it damned nuclear power plants and questioned their safety. The document turned out to be an unfinished study based on outdated data, and it was so "secret" that it had been discussed in a speech by William O. Doub, an AEC official. When Doub challenged Nader and "other unreasoning critics of nuclear technology" to a debate "based on precise facts, not overstated generalities," Nader carefully side-stepped the opportunity to show up the "conspiracy" he so frequently charged or to present his views in a forum other than one dominated by the environmentalist claque.*

When Nader discussed radioactive waste, it was almost always in terms of the 115,000 gallons of high-level waste which leaked out of a holding tank at the Hanford AEC installation in Washing-

*Nader has always avoided facing those he has attacked, or admitting error. In *Vanishing Air*, one of his reports, Senator Edmund Muskie was dismissed as a blatant hypocrite who put his political interests above those of the environmentalist cause. Called to task by a reporter, Nader said, "I'll call up Muskie—about something else." He never did.

ton State. Unwary listeners were made to feel that this waste had seeped into the Columbia River where it was threatening the lives of people and radioactively destroying the environment The unwary could never learn the true state of affairs from Nader, although the facts were all at hand. They were described by Dixy Lee Ray in an interview with *U.S. News & World Report*, published in November 1973:

> Thirty years ago when this facility was built, these big holding tanks were the best answer to the question, "What are we going to do with the stuff?" It was never expected that these tanks would last forever. They anticipated that the corrosive, hot, high-level radioactive waste would indeed corrode the tanks and perhaps seep into the soil unless they were replaced periodically . . . The waste that has leaked from these tanks is not endangering anybody because of absorption by the soil and small amounts of rainfall.
>
> Back in 1965, we started a program to solidy or evaporate this material, turning it into a solid we call "salt cakes." By 1976, most of it should be in solid form. This has one advantage: It doesn't leak . . .
>
> Q. How long would it take this leaked waste material to reach the Columbia River?
>
> A. If it reaches the water table, and if you allow 1,500 years, it will get into the Columbia River. But by that time, the natural half-life of these materials would have disarmed most of them and the rest would have been naturally absorbed in the soil.
>
> There is less radioactivity in the Columbia River—the same river we take water from for the Hanford program—than in the Potomac River from natural causes.

"Environmental improvement used to be a scientific and technical problem," environmental consultant Perry A. Miller has written. "But it's changed from a problem of applied knowledge to a problem of applied politics." This is something Nader has known all along. Applied knowledge says, as does Dr. Lapp: "I see nuclear power . . . as the only practicable energy source in sight adequate to sustain our way of life and to promote our economy." Applied politics says, as does Ralph Nader, that we can dispense with nuclear energy and turn to solar heat—though the scientists have shown that to replace a utility burning 9,000 tons of coal a day would require "a collection area of 18 million square yards to absorb the necessary solar heat" (Lapp's words). Assuming that this heat can be "converted to electric power at 30 percent efficiency, this would mean paving over 20 square miles with solar catchers" to duplicate the 9,000 tons of coal. When Nader argued that this kind of heat could supply half the nation's energy needs by 1985, in a bitter exchange with members of the Joint Atomic Energy Committee, Representative Mike McCormack answered: "That's the most absurd statement made here today." Then returning to Nader talk of nuclear hazards, McCormack snapped: "What we're picking up here in cigarette smoke in this room is more hazardous than all the radioactivity we will get from nuclear power."

But applied politics rules the Nader roost. After a visit to Hawaii in which he chatted with a group of university students, J. Davitt McAteer, a Nader Raider, wrote a four-page pamphlet which Nader widely distributed to airlines, steamship offices, and travel agencies. The pamphlet charged that Hawaii's air was heavy with pollution, the beaches were excessively overcrowded, raw sewage was being pumped into the ocean in dangerous quantities, and pesticide concentration was ten times that of the mainland. Investigation showed that Hawaiian air was considerably purer than that of any mainland state, with Honolulu having the lowest rate of any major American city, that McAteer had grossly exaggerated the crowds on the beaches, and that the dumping of sewage in the ocean was strictly monitored.

But for Nader, it was simply a case of environmentalism *uber alles.*

Environmentalism, however, must be as environmentalism does. "We've got to understand that going all out 'to stop pollution' will be harmful to the environment," Perry Miller wrote in *Industry Week* magazine. "For today we're failing to consider the requirements we're placing upon air, water, land, and energy to meet our arbitrarily and scientifically meaningless pollution requirements. We've allowed ourselves to become so preoccupied with 'pollution' that we're ignoring the environment and we're ignoring conservation."

By demanding "zero pollution"—a total impossibility—Nader took the leap into all-out denunciation of nuclear power, the cleanest and least damaging to the environment. To justify this position, he argued that anything beyond thirty-nine nuclear power plants in the United States would mean suicide. The country has far exceeded that number, and is pushing toward the thousand plants which will soon supply us with more than 50 percent of our energy needs. Nader also insisted that nuclear energy for peaceful uses was "through" because of its inefficiency and because of its hazards—a statement which led Dr. Chauncey Starr, a nuclear physicist who had also served as dean of the University of California in Los Angeles, to describe Nader as an "ignoramus" and an "enemy of society." And to add, "When a man becomes a god-hero, he no longer recognizes the limit of his own powers. Nader is just as greedy for public power as some politicians are."

Nader's antinuclear passions lost him the respect of the scientific community. He did not help matters when he blurted out, "The use of solar energy has not been opened up because the oil industry does not own the sun."

12

A Nader Potpourri

WHAT FOLLOWS IS PART OF A LONG MEMORANDUM, PREPARED by a highly reliable source on Capitol Hill who had, with growing astonishment, watched the rise of Ralph Nader. It is reproduced here much as it was written, though some of the raw indignation has been deleted and comments have been added in square brackets. Some names have been deleted to protect the innocent.

* * * *

Forgive me Nader, though I know what I am doing. For a number of years, I have been watching you operating on and off the Hill. I have also committed one terrible sin, namely collecting clippings on your activities. I realize that where you are concerned it is *lèse majesté* to hold you accountable for what you say and do, so forgive me. Let me put it this way:

The girl in question was no novice to Washington nor to the ways of Capitol Hill. Admittedly, her existence on the staff of Representative————had not always been pleasant. But on quitting her job, she said very little about her difficulties with him, and that only to a few close friends. When Ralph Nader launched his Congress Project, her interest was little more than academic. So she was quite unprepared for the phone call that took her out of a staff meeting with the professional organization at which she worked.

"Miss————? I'm with Ralph Nader's Congress Project. I understand you were once administrative assistant to Congressman————?"

"I was," she answered. "I'm not any longer, and have no connections with his office."

"I'd like to ask you, Miss————————what sexual demands did Congressman————————make on female members of his staff?"

She held her temper in check long enough to reply quietly that she did not care to discuss any aspect of her previous employment.

Gary Sellers had two years with the Washington law firm of Covington & Burling, and moved from there to the Bureau of the Budget, at which time he met Nader. In 1969, Sellers left a law job with a former senator to work for Nader—at Nader's request. Sellers had been working on the Coal Mine Health and Safety Act, in which Nader was deeply involved. While on Nader's payroll, lobbying for a coal bill, Sellers also went to work for Representative Phillip Burton, a California Democrat, who was on a House subcommittee handling that bill. Sellers is quoted in *Citizen Nader* as saying that he was receiving only a "minimal salary" from both. [During his first year with Nader, he received $10,000.] That's not quite the point. Part III of the Code of Official Conduct of the House of Representatives is admittedly awkwardly written but certainly it applies to Sellers' action:

> A member, officer, or employee of the House of Representatives shall receive no compensation to accrue to his beneficial interest from any source, the receipt of which would occur by virtue of influence improperly exerted from his position in the Congress.

If the House Committee of Official Conduct were asked an advisory opinion on the ethics of double employment, particularly where a piece of controversial legislation was involved, they would say it ran counter to both the letter and the spirit of the code. Sellers told McCarry, author of *Citizen Nader:*

> I was also working for Ralph. Sure I was. If someone wants to think that's a conflict of loyalty or ethics, let 'em. Goddam it, I didn't do it for my employer, I did it for myself. If they want to prosecute me, let them try.

[According to Nader, both he and Burton were fully aware of Sellers' double role.]

I'm sure you know all about Nader's attacks on Paul Rand Dixon, chairman of the Federal Trade Commission, and his practice of slipping a blast to the press without letting Dixon know about it, so that he could make no rebuttal when the papers called him. I'm sure you also know of the statement made by Charles McCarry after Nader had seen the manuscript of *Citizen Nader:* "In twenty years of reporting, I have never encountered anything that compared to the kind of harassment and intimidation that I've gotten on this book."

This is no secret to those of us on the Hill. Congressmen and senators who cooperated with Nader on some of his projects and who gave him status—Abe Ribicoff of Connecticut is one such— find themselves under vicious attack if they depart a few degrees from Nader's direction. Suddenly the political gossip columnists are being fed nasty items about these men and the whispering campaign begins. Nader deplores secrecy, but at one point he had a corps of spies both in the executive branch and among the staff members of congressional committees, all doing their best to disrupt the orderly workings of government in order to give Ralph a headline. How can anyone of us do our work when we aren't sure that the guy next to us isn't taking notes to give to Nader. He has loudly deplored the Watergate burglars and the plumbers, charging immorality and a violation of civil rights. But those on Nader's enemies list don't stand a prayer.

Look what happened to William Haddon, Jr., the first head of the National Traffic Safety Agency. Haddon had worked closely with Nader and his appointment was applauded by the "consumer advocate." But he made it clear that he was his own man and would not be dominated by Nader. Shortly after Haddon's agency had issued its first set of automobile safety standards, Nader accused it of having sold out to Detroit. He also smeared Haddon through Drew Pearson by feeding him an item that an industry representative was "an old friend and MIT alumnus of Haddon's" —though the two men had barely known each other at MIT. Nader also publicly complained to Haddon that his agency was doing nothing about Volkswagen gas caps which "loosen or disengage during collisions." Yet he knew at the time of his complaint that Haddon had taken steps to correct that situation.

While commenting on Nader's ethical sense, there's the case of another attack he made on the Volkswagen, slipped to John D. Morris at a *New York Times* evening party at its Washington bureau. The story was hardly accurate and highly overblown, and even Morris, who adores Nader, was forced to concede that "Ralph's story made it sound like it was a national scandal, and the truth of the matter was that it involved just one or two cases. I've never known Nader deliberately to say anything that isn't true, but he gets a little careless with his facts sometimes and he should be checked out . . . He's liable to float something just to see if it's true."

Well, Nader tried to float that story, but when it sank, he never apologized or explained—and he included it in his report on the Federal Trade Commission in 1969—which raises questions about how deliberate he is when he gets "careless." The Nader morality is pretty flexible, as he showed clearly when his lawyer was able to pry loose a White House tape. The lawyer, William A Dobrivir, took the tape home and played it at a cocktail party. And what did Nader say about this? At first, silence. Then, when ABC tracked him down, he brushed the episode aside as an "unfortunate excess," and he refused to fire Dobrivir. As John Lofton, who used to work here on the Hill, said, "Unlike Richard Nixon, Ralph Nader is keeping his John Dean on the job."

There's an old German saying, *Kein Engel ist so rein*—no angel is so pure—but perhaps it should be changed to *Kein Nader ist so rein*. Certainly, no angel is so busy as Nader.

Because many members of Congress once got considerable numbers of letters echoing Nader charges, I've kept a clip file on him. When you flip through it, you are astounded by his complete lack of loyalty to anyone, as well as by his ingratitude. Here are some soundings.

On November 2, 1967, President Lyndon Johnson, in a speech, paid tribute to Nader's sensibility to the nation's needs. Just two months later, Nader accused LBJ of an "outrageous" sellout to the auto industry.

In June 1972, Nader accused the Internal Revenue Service of issuing a ruling that "seems tailor-made to immunize from gift-tax liability donations made to" President Nixon's reelection committee. [This is truly ingratitude, since IRS has never questioned Nader on the lobbying and political activities of his tax-exempt organizations—barred by law from such activities—or slapped him across the wrist when these organizations have filed their information returns months late.]

Also in June 1972, Nader issued a report on the civil service system, charging that our civil servants were badly treated and not given the advancement they deserved. Yet Nader told a student audience at Georgetown University that most civil servants are "to put it mildly, drones . . . They really believe that they . . . have

thirty years of experience instead of what most of them really have
—one year of experience repeated thirty times."

Early in July 1972, Nader paid a visit to Australia, and liter-
ally before he had a chance to change his underpants had issued a "report" criticizing that country's auto safety and libel
laws. Prime Minister William McMahon, not being subject to
the fear of Nader suffered by our own officials, dismissed him
as "a professional and paid pot-stirrer"—pot-stirrer being the
Australian term for troublemaker. "He," said the prime minister, "has been in Australia for twenty-four hours"—the truth
was closer to four hours— "and he has set himself up as a
judge of Australia without proper knowledge of the country
and its people. Nader will be paid normal courtesies as a
visitor, but an Australian who went to America and made the
same criticisms would not be well received."

The Australians had their revenge. They quoted Nader accurately when, in a speech, he recommended "socialism or communism" as the solution to the country's putative ills. Nader did not
deny the quote when it appeared in Australia. But when it was
picked up by *Barron's*, he wrote a violent letter attacking the
writer as a "journalistic coward" and ranting of "archaic balder-
dash," "libels and labels," "ideological excess and slovenly research," though never categorically denying that he had said what
he was reported to have said.

Sometimes members of Congress are criticized by their constituents for not objecting to some of the more outrageous
things Nader says. But to object you have to keep up with this
now-you-see-it-now-you-don't man—and that's next to impossible. One newsmagazine has put a ban on criticism of Nader because it would "hurt the cause"—a journalistic approach shared
by the *Washington Post* and the *New York Times*. But a ran-
dom selection of headlines raises the question: What cause?
Read 'em:

"Nader Forms Unit to Aid Crusaders for Public" (*Washington
Post*, June 2, 1971)

"Nader Accuses USDA of Allowing Bad Meat" (*Washington Post*,
July 18, 1971)

"Nader Mobilizes Retired Professionals to Tackle Problems of
Social Change" (*New York Times*, July 28, 1972)

"Housing Quality Seen Top Issue by Nader" (*Washington Post*,
April 7, 1972)

"Nader Says Schools Lag on Issues" (*Washington Post*, May 11, 1972)*

"Nader Sees Small Claims Court Defects" (*Washington Post*, June 14, 1972)

"Nader Seeks Fining of CAB Members on Pair of Petitions" (*Wall Street Journal*, June 23, 1972)

"Banks Control Big Airlines, Complaint by Nader Charges" (*Washington Post*, July 7, 1972)

"Nader Calls Press 'Mirror of Nixon'" (*Washington Star*, December 15, 1972) [This was the laugh of the week]

"Nader Asks EPA to Investigate Asbestos Danger" (*Washington Star*, January 3, 1973)

"Nader Group Asks CAB to Set Atlantic Fare at $125 for One Way" (*Wall Street Journal*, January 3, 1973)

All of this and Nader's bulky mailing pieces, full of self-praise and asking for money on the basis of a self-evaluation of his achievements. The last such mailing we got at this office included a twenty-four page pamphlet entitled *Public Citizen Report No. 2*, which nowhere told his readers what Nader did with the millions of dollars he has collected from them.

But no matter. What disturbs many of us working on the Hill the most is Nader's silence about something that strikes at the very core of Congress freedom to act independently. Nader frequently attacks the business lobby, but he says nothing about the most powerful lobby in Washington. I mean, of course, the Big Labor lobby. The AFL-CIO contributed millions of dollars in cash to the election campaigns of senators and would-be senators, of congressmen and would-be congressmen. The last time I checked, I discovered that Senator Birch Bayh of Indiana received $70,000 in cash from Big Labor. Representative Peter Rodino received more than $30,000. These sums represent cash and do not include the invaluable and costly help they got from people on the union payroll, or the bills picked up by individual unions for candidates they supported. When Andy Biemiller, the AFL-CIO chief lobbyist, or any of his assistants goes from office to office twisting arms to get a bill passed, he gets the kind of attention the big corporations would give a small fortune to get.

*This one deserves comment. In a speech to several hundred "reform-minded" educators, Nader advised that they give up the teaching of civics and study supermarket prices, advertising jingles, and the property tax as "a beautiful way" to teach government to students.

Nader won't attack Big Labor because he knows that if George Meany or the United Auto Workers turned on him they could cut him to pieces. He could really raise hell with Congress and labor about "conflict of interest" or how the unions have been able to prevent passage of many bills that might hurt the big boys, no matter how much it would help rank-and-file union members. All the polls show that a majority of the country—including union families—oppose compulsory unionism and would like a national right-to-work law, but you'll never hear Nader say a word about this.

Very little has been written about Nader's machine on the Hill, and what kind of "conflict of interest" that causes. A couple of years back a study was made of Nader's underground in Congress. It merely touched the high points and some of the people named have left. But the muscle is still there. As I recall, the study pointed out that Senator Gaylord Nelson, chairman of the Senate Small Business and Monopoly Subcommittee, and Representative Benjamin S. Rosenthal are directors of Nader's Center for Auto Safety—which may account for the dismal quality of some of the legislation enacted in this field.

National Journal noted at the time that "a small coterie of Capitol Hill employees work closely" with Nader and the Raiders. That was back in 1971, before the Congress Project aroused the members and before Nader began insulting them right and left during public hearings. But he was doing pretty well when he had under his influence and carrying water for him the following:

James Flug, chief counsel to the Senate Judiciary Subcommittee on Administrative Practice and Procedure, headed by Senator Edward M. Kennedy

Jack A. Blum, assistant counsel to the Senate Judiciary Subcommittee on Antitrust and Monopoly Legislation, headed by Senator Philip A. Hart

Michael Pertschuk, chief counsel to the Senate Commerce Committee, headed by Senator Warren G. Magnuson

Kenneth A. McLean, professional staff member of the Senate Banking, Housing, and Urban Affairs Committee, headed by Senator John Sparkman

Martin Lobel, former law professor and now legislative assistant to Senator William A. Proxmire

And it hasn't hurt Nader to have among his "coterie" in the Executive Branch someone like William Howard Taft, IV, who was a special assistant to Caspar Weinberger when he was deputy director of the Office of Management and Budget, and who moved with Weinberger to the Department of Health, Education, and Welfare when W. became the secretary. You can ask yourself who it was who leaked a report made by the U.S. Army Corps of Engineers for the OMB on the costs of eliminating water pollution. Nader used that report to fire a blast at the OMB for "holding up" release of the report, delivering his letter to the press, natch, long before the OMB had received its copy.

We continue to get communications from Nader about this or that, but we were all amused when one of his assistants circularized the members of Congress and, for all I know, half the executive branch. The letter read in part:

> Ralph Nader has always felt that the average visitor to our nation's capital is given short shrift when it comes to getting *involved* as a citizen. He is offered ample opportunity to become a "gawker" —by means of the tourmobile and other packaged tourist techniques, he sees *exteriors* of beautiful buildings and monuments . . .
>
> To partially rectify this situation, Public Citizen is opening a Visitors Center . . . on May 15th [1974]. The purpose of this [PCVC] will be to make the tourist issue-oriented and consumer-conscious. To accomplish these goals, he will be offered a diversity of choices for "off the beaten path" participation in local and federal activities —all the while allowing him to have fun and relaxation as he engages in new, relevant experiences . . .
>
> May we request your cooperation, also, in making your facilities available to the PCVC? . . . If our "typical visitor" can return to his home-town community with a maximum of meaningful, jointly-contributed data, we hope he or she will put this knowledge to work for the benfit of all . . .

It was meaningful all right. The program for one of the PCVC's first weeks in business added to the tourist's consumer-consciousness and "participation" in the issues by showing him movies of Ralph Nader, other movies prepared by the AFL-CIO, a tour of the

FBI which is taken by almost every visitor to Washington, and a discussion of homosexuality.

This is how the contributions of those who look to Nader with adultation are being used.

If you want an idea of how many congressmen feel about Ralph Nader, you don't have to do a big research job. Just turn to the *Congressional Record* for October 3, 1972, page H9062, and read what Representative Clarence Brown of Ohio has to say.

The *Congressional Record* cited includes these remarks by Brown of Ohio:

> Mr. BROWN of Ohio. . . . The reference [to me in *Who Runs Congress?*] occurs on page 140 in a discussion of the scurrilous conflicts of interest which Mr. Nader would like the American public to believe haunt each of the members of this body. I am cited as currently owning a radio station in my hometown while at the same time serving on the Communications Subcommittee of the Interstate and Foreign Commerce Committee. The fact Mr. Nader and friends omitted to point out was that this station was sold by me two years ago and I retain no interest in it at all . . . FCC regulations prohibit the sale of a radio station for three years after it is put on the air. [Brown had put the station on the air prior to his election to Congress.] So it was not until 1969 that I could legally divest myself of it, and the sale was consummated early in 1970.
>
> If nothing else, one would have expected that Mr. Nader would have called me or the radio station or the Federal Communications Commission before going to press with his inaccurate information. He did not.
>
> The matter is all the more curious, however, because more than a month and a half ago during the personal interview to which I submitted with Nader's Congress Project reporters, they brought the same charge up and I set the record straight then. . . .
>
> If Ralph Nader has any doubt about the reason why the vast majority of members of Congress hold him in low esteem, he need look no farther than the hogwash printed in his own book. As I said earlier, it is only a taste of what is to come, so settle back for a good laugh. The congressional watchdog has been caught catnapping.

13

Naderism, Consumerism, and Muckraking

IT HAS BEEN SAID OF RALPH NADER THAT HIS IDEA OF THE perfect state is one in which lawyers dominate all phases of life. His advice, always, is to sue—and he has made himself one of the most litigious men in America. Others have said that had he more weight and more muscle, he would have become a professional barroom brawler. The insult comes quick to his lips, and with it the imputation that whoever disagrees with him is a fool, a thief, or a rogue. His respect for lawyers, however, remains constant. When the American Trial Lawyers Association came out against no-fault insurance, Nader, who had begun beating the drums for it, backed off. There was, of course, some acrimony when the *New Republic* disclosed that the ATLA had made a $10,000 contribution to Nader's Center for Auto Safety, but in the rather shabby controversy that followed Nader said it was all a lie and the money was returned.

It would, however, be inaccurate to overstress Nader's penchant for the class action suit which damages the defendant, enriches the legal profession, and usually leaves the plaintiffs with little more than a sense of achievement. In any case, the Supreme Court has struck a blow at class action litigation. It would be a mistake, as well, to think of Nader in terms of financial gain. For though he has gathered unto himself an unknown number of millions of dollars for which he has never accounted, and runs the business side of his life with unparalled secrecy, he has also spent a considerable amount of money. The dollar for him is a weapon to be used against those who have amassed the hard cash which makes the wheels of industry turn.

To understand Ralph Nader and his impact on the country it is important to place him in the context of the consumerist movement, of the muckraking tradition, and of the New Left's onslaught on the nation's social and political values. In relation to the last category, it is interesting that when the New Leftists were casting about for a presidential candidate in 1972, their first choice was Nader. He wisely rejected that dubious honor for it would have destroyed him as a consumerist. But Benjamin Spock, Gloria Steinem, and Gore Vidal saw him as one of their own—and though he bowed away from so open a political role, he took no umbrage at the embrace. Yet Nader's identification with the New Left has been more apparent than real. That movement has a broad anarchist streak in it, and it is self-indulgent in ways that Nader finds repugnant. In temperament, Nader is authoritarian, which explains his occasional kind words for socialism and communism. But on the surface at least, the ideological outgrowths of Marxism are antielitist, antitechnocratic, and suspicious of fanatics in overdrive.

The lifestyle of the New Left also runs counter to Nader's. The free-and-easy sex *mores* offend Nader's asceticism, and if driven to the wall, he would probably argue that sexual encounters be limited solely to procreation—and even there carefully restricted by government to enforce zero population growth. He would also argue that sex is a waste of time. The use of drugs, from marijuana to the hard, upsets a man who considers even the drinking of Coca-Cola a crime against humanity.

If Nader ever stopped running long enough to organize his ideological beliefs, to put them in systematic order, he would come up with something very much akin to what Benito Mussolini called "corporatism"—from which the "corporate state" of Italian fascism derived. Ideally, under fascism, industry was a functioning troika of government, owners (or managers), and the "people." Mussolini quickly substituted members of the *fascisti*, which meant the government, for the "people"—so that management survived only if it bowed subserviently to government power.

Nader has fought for popular, by which he means "consumerist," representation on the boards of directors of all the big corporations, on pain of government sanctions. But consumerist to him does not mean consumer-oriented. It means those who accept his own philosophy wholeheartedly. After all, we are all consumers, and among us there are many who are still bigoted enough to cleave to the vanishing ways of a free-market economy. Should the day come when Nader's dream of all-powerful regulatory agencies, staffed by his adherents, are sanctioned by law, Nader would turn away from his insistence on consumerist representation in the affairs of business and industry—as his speeches and writings have indicated.

If Nader should have his way—if Congress ever gives him the kind of Consumer Protective Agency he has demanded—then the United States will have moved a giant step in the direction of the kind of state he sees as the wave of the future. For the CPA, as envisioned by Nader, would have more power than the Justice Department and the White House combined in all matters except foreign policy. No decision of the Congress or the executive branch would have the color of law if challenged by the CPA. It would have the right to intervene in the affairs of all agencies, regulatory or otherwise, all departments, and all acts of the national legislature if, in its wisdom, it decided that these in any way impinged on the consumer and his putative rights. Even a new weapons system devised by the Pentagon could run into CPA estoppel if that super-government decided that its cost would increase the taxes paid by consumers. And the CPA would have a right to take any arm of government into court to enforce its decisions. It could also direct industry priorities, prices, wages, new-product decisions, and environmental matters—since these touched on the life of the "consumer"—a kind of American Politburo.

To satisfy Nader, the Consumer Protective Agency would have to be dedicated to his own view of what is best for a stupid consumer who likes to "waste" time watching football games on television, who spends billions on cigarettes and liquor and cosmetics, and who insists on eating foods not as nutritional as soybeans, wheat germ, and yogurt. That millions of Americans like Wonder Bread or Wheaties is an abomination to Nader, and one he would quickly delete from the American life style. The culprit to him in this is advertising, which he would so restrict that there would be little point for industry to spend money on promoting its products. What this would do to the jobs and incomes of the media people who have made a national hero of Nader is easy to guess. Eventually, it would destroy the printed and electronic press, which could not survive for a day without the infusions of corporate money which make our daily newspapers, magazines, and TV radio programs possible. Without advertising, the media could exist only if subsidized by government, which would destroy both the freedom—and license—they now enjoy and reduce them to propaganda arms of the party in power.

Just how conscious Nader may be of the implications of what he proposes is a real question. There is no question of Nader's consuming hatred for the business and industry which conquered a continent and, in its own unmotivated way, gave the United States the highest standard of living in the history of man—a hatred which, perhaps, should be submitted to the analysis of Freudian psychiatry since, as so many observers have noted, there is some sexual twist to the propelling force in Nader's psyche. There is little doubt that, however much Nader may bring palpitations to adolescent girls and aging spinsters, the usual sexual interests fail to vibrate in him. (Though they wished to storm Jerusalem, Richard the Lion-Hearted had his boys and the Crusaders their girls.) The conclusions of such a Freudian inquiry, however, would only be a side-bar to any understanding of Nader, Naderism, and their role.

Ralph Nader enjoys being described as a muckraker. But his relationship to the muckraking of the early twentieth century is, at the very most, tangential. The similarities are there, but they are more apparent than real, though there is considerable parallelism. In 1906, David Graham Phillips sought to alarm the country with his *The Treason of the Senate*. In 1972, Nader's Congress Project produced the scissors-and-paste *Who Runs Congress?* Ida Tarbell published *The History of the Standard Oil Company* in 1902. In 1971, Nader issued his whimsical and unfactual attack on DuPont. *The Great American Fraud* was Samuel Hopkins Adams' 1905 riposte to the producers of patent medicine. Sixty-six years later, in a small paperback called *Beware*, Nader anguished over the alleged thousands of deaths, injuries, and hospitalizations "due in large part to the nature of the manufacture and improper use of products which because of inadequate and oftimes antiquated product safety standards . . . speciously [*sic*] sanction this outrage to be suffered by the public." Thomas W. Lawson's *Frenzied Finance* took on the great trusts in 1904. Nader returned to the same theme in 1971, 1972, and 1973, in a series of reports and books— some of which bore his name and all his imprimatur. William Hard wept over the plight of the American newsboy, and Nader raised the ante by charging that for every single member of the American labor force "there is no such thing as an interesting job."

But, as a rule, the old muckrakers worked hard to get their facts, to research their subjects. And they worked and wrote as individuals. If the public responded, that was their reward. But they did not incorporate themselves into a movement, did not recruit underpaid young people to fight the battle, and did not solicit funds by direct mail and newspaper advertising which were squirreled away with no accountability. However astringently they might attack abuses in the society, they were not ascetic zealots, lacking in all the usual human juices—and they got along with their fellow men.

As historian Richard Hofstadter noted, "Their criticisms of American society were, in their utmost reaches, very searching and radical, but they were themselves moderate men who intended to propose no radical remedies." Ray Stannard Baker could say of himself and of other muckrakers, "We 'muckraked' not because we hated our world but because we loved it. We were not cynical, we were not bitter." There were some extremist muckrakers, but William Allen White, a social critic and journalist of considerable standing, dismissed them, describing "the pale drawn face, the set lips, and a general line of insanity" in those who saw muckraking as the fulcrum of destruction. This same theme was echoed by Theodore Roosevelt, popularizer of the term, who warned that "the men with the muckrakes are often indispensable to the well-being of society, but only when they know when to stop raking the muck and look upward to the celestial crown above them, to the crown of worthy endeavor"—imagery he took from *Pilgrim's Progress.* "If they grow to feel that the whole world is nothing but muck, their power of usefulness is gone."

Then as now, what passes for "muckraking" could be highly profitable. Ida Tarbell received $4,000 for each of her famous articles, and Lincoln Steffens got $2,000—sums which translated into 1970s dollars compare more than favorably with the fees Nader receives for his lectures and for magazine pieces which he sometimes writes himself. But the old muckrakers lacked Nader's ability to tap the great reservoir of the tax-exempt foundations and to receive six-figure contributions from the very industrialists he is out to decimate. The old muckrakers also enjoyed a sense of humor. Steffens recalls in his autobiography how an astute use of statistics, planted in scare stories, could convince the citizenry that it was living in the midst of a horrendous crime wave:

> I enjoy crime waves. I made one once . . . Many reporters joined in the uplift of the rising tide of crime . . . I feel I know something the wise men do not know about crime waves and get a certain

sense of happy superiority out of reading editorials, sermons, speeches, and learned theses on my specialty . . . Police records showed no increase at all; on the contrary the totals of crime showed a diminution. It was only the newspaper reports of crime that increased."

It would be impossible to conceive of a muckraking Nader conceding that his fiery denunciations of a choking increase of air pollution, picked up by editorial writers, was simply another "crime wave"—that the actual statistics showed a steady decline in urban air pollution from the time records were kept—and that this diminution has not increased in pace since he and the environmentalists began their long chant.

When Upton Sinclair, in a wheelchair, and Ralph Nader met at the White House in 1967 to witness the signing by President Lyndon Johnson of the Wholesome Meat Act—a piece of legislation for which Nader took the hog's share of credit but which he now admits worsened conditions—history presumably came full circle. Sinclair, who in his own words had "aimed at the public's heart and by accident hit it in the stomach," was the author of the 1906 sensation, *The Jungle,* an exposé of the meat-packing industry which almost turned the country to vegetarianism and led to substantial reforms. Nader's *The Waste Lords* made use of the same shock approach in an attempt to convince Americans that their environment was unspeakably foul and the fault of the corporate beast. In his overblown introduction Nader wrote what, unlike Sinclair, he could never justify.

> Knowing and unremitting destruction of rivers and their usefulness to human beings, contamination of the air that people draw into their lungs, scarring the land with poisons and debris, the impairment of people's health and property with total immunity and . . . a massive taxpayer's subsidy for so doing, are macabre portraits that can be drawn for many cities and towns in this country.

Lincoln Steffens and Ida Tarbell would have laughed at this rhetoric and barred Nader from the muckraking club. But what of Nader as consumerist? Almost every news story about him bears the descriptive term, "consumer advocate"—a phrase even used by editorialists taking exception to his activities. Nader, in fact, seeks to create the impression that he is somehow the father of

consumerism—though some of the diatribes by Erasmus, the six-
teenth-century philosopher and humanist, against the cheating of
merchants and the shoddy goods they purveyed matches Nader's
more virulent outbursts, and President John F. Kennedy's assault
on all businessmen as "sons of bitches" long before Nader came on
the scene is part of our recent history. In fact, organized consumerism came into being long before Nader was born, when F. J.
Schlink founded Consumers' Research, an organization which
tested products and reported on them to its members.

Consumers' Research pointed its lance at individual malprac-
tices in industry and business, not at industry and business *per se.*
Even Consumers' Union, which was born after a violent and unsuccessful strike against CR in the mid-1930s led by unsuccessful
Communist infiltrators, stressed product value though it took
strong political positions.* Its publications struck out at what it
called our "junk society" and urged readers to join the "struggle"
against a corrupt society, but CU's major appeal was to people who
wanted to know what consumer products were better than others,
how to make purchases, how to avoid being cheated, and other
matters of strictly consumer interest. Ralph Nader's consumerist
beginnings were with Consumers' Union, on whose board of directors he sits, and *Unsafe At Any Speed* quoted frequently from CU
reports.

What Ralph Nader did, when his battle with General Motors
made him a public figure, was to take CU's implicit position and
make it explicit, all in the context of his natural militancy and
activism. To make consumerism political, he employed the agit-
prop approach of the '30s, launching a broad-scale attack on all
phases of the American economic system and the market
economy, for which he blamed every product shortcoming as an
inevitable result. The large and evil American corporations, he
argued from the start, "are able to divert scarce resources to uses

*Consumers' Union was headed for many years by Arthur Kallet (party name,
Edward Adams), author with Schlink of the best-selling *100,000,000 Guinea Pigs,*
whose affiliation with the Communist movement was so open that it was decried
by Arthur M. Schlesinger, Jr., in his book, *The Coming of the New Deal.* CU itself
was cited as a Communist front by such organizations as the House Appropriations
Committee, the Pennsylvania Commonwealth Council, a committee of the New
York City Council, the House Committee on Un-American Activities, etc., until
1953 when, after secret hearings never published, it was "cleared" by the HCUA.
A recital of the affiliations and public statements of communists and procommu-
nists who ran CU would serve little purpose in this account.

that have little human benefit or are positively harmful." A corollary of this value judgment was the flat statement that consumers today can no longer determine the value of what they buy or its usefulness, that they are at the mercy of Madison Avenue and the greedy producers, and that they can be protected only by the "tiny *ad hoc* coalitions of determined people" which he controlled.*

If a particular car is a "lemon," it is, to Nader, proof positive of a conspiracy in the board rooms of Detroit and not, as the *Washington Post* surprisingly noted in a series of articles, because workers on the assembly line—protected by their union—smoke marijuana at their work. Corporate abuse, as Professor Ralph K. Winter, Jr., pointed out in a study of *The Consumer Advocate Versus the Consumer,* written for the nonpartisan American Enterprise Institute for Public Policy Research,

> is assumed to exist and the burden of proving otherwise is put upon those who dare to deny it, with the strong implication that a denial is evidence of one's indifference to the ills of society. Consumer advocates tend to toss off a lot of quotations and statistics but when one culls "estimates" and polemical arguments from verifiable fact, their work product seems far too thin to be taken as an assessment of a trillion dollar economy.
>
> Skepticism as the scientific basis of consumerism's factual premises, for example, are not discouraged by the liberality with which Mr. Nader and lesser movers of the cause employ Senator [Philip] Hart's estimate of $200 billion of consumer abuse. But $200 billion seems substantially in excess of total profits for all business and almost four times total after-tax corporate profits.
>
> . . . When Mr. Nader criticizes the food industry for taking steps to "sharpen and meet superficially consumer tastes at the cost of other critical consumer needs," one may fairly ask whose judgment it is that a taste is "superficial" and whose judgment it is that a "need" is "critical." In the circumstances mentioned it seems rather evident that the judgment in question is solely Mr. Nader's.

This was put in another way by an economist, the late Frank H. Knight, who suggested that

*"The 'consumer movement,' as it is sometimes called, isn't really a movement, and has never really caught on among ordinary people," James Ridgeway has written in the radical *Hard Times,* "perhaps because of the muddy politics involved . . . Almost inevitably, consumer protection becomes a game among elite groups."

136

A large part of the critics' strictures on the existing system come down to protests against the individual wanting what he wants instead of what is good for him, of which the critic is to be judge; and the critic does not feel himself called upon even to outline any standards other than his own preferences upon a basis of which judgment is to be passed.

The "abuses" take many forms. For many years, Nader's consumerists held it as an article of faith that manufacturers of dry foods shortweighted their packages, hiding this by using deceptively large boxes. A Food and Drug Administration survey made in 1973, however, showed that these packages were "overfilled by about 4 percent of their declared net weight"—with candies overfilled an average of 8 percent. The survey received little notice, and housewives, still convinced by Nader that Erasmus was right when he said that merchants "will lie, perjure themselves, steal, cheat, and mislead the public"—which many indeed did when he lived in Holland way back then—will tell you that they are being shortweighted. And Congress, prodded by Nader's elitists, seemed to feel the same. During its ninety-second session, more than five hundred bills were introduced—all "consumer" legislation "hobbling what is left of free enterprise," according to *Barron's*.

These hundreds of bills will be enacted only if the Nader "movement" continues to lobby for them. But what will they achieve? The regulatory agencies that Nader advocates usually end up sticking the consumer. For example, the Civil Aeronautics Board, which regulates all interstate flights, also sets prices. But CAB-"regulated" fares average some 74 percent higher than intrastate nonregulated fares. Dr. Theodore F. Keeler of the University of California, Berkeley, made some tabulations—and this was before interstate fares had been sharply increased. At that time, a New York-Washington flight cost $24.07, whereas the comparable distance in intrastate flight cost $14.96, or 50 percent less. Los Angeles to Reno, under the "protectionist" CAB, cost $39.63, whereas a comparable intrastate flight cost $15.28, or 116 percent less. Flying the distance from Miami to New York on intrastate, unregulated lines cost $84 percent less.

The government regulation that Nader wants does more harm than good, as anyone who has ridden on our railroads knows. And now the Federal Trade Commission, bending to Nader's demands for greater militancy in behalf of the consumer, has promulgated what it calls an "unfairness doctrine." The FTC's Food and Drug Advertising Division has announced that even businesses whose advertising is absolutely truthful will by prosecuted if an FTC bureaucrat decides that its *intent* is to take unfair advantage of some unspecified consumer weakness. Under the "unfairness doctrine" the FTC filed a complaint against Wonder Bread's advertising slogan that its product "Helps Build Strong Bodies 12 Ways." The FTC conceded that this was a true statement. But it suspected that other breads might do the same, and demanded that Wonder Bread so note in its advertisements.

But Nader goes far beyond this. According to the Associated Press, he told a Providence, Rhode Island, audience that "corporations that abuse the public interest should be transferred to public trusteeship and their officers sent to jail"—in other words, socialized. Given Nader's definition of "public interest" as spelled out in his report on DuPont, this would mean the nationalization of all American industry. Thomas Shepard, who was publisher of *Look*, commented,

> The syllogism is inescapable. Ralph Nader says corporations that abuse the public interest should be taken over by the government. According to Ralph Nader, virtually all corporations abuse the public interest. Therefore, all corporations should be taken over by the government.

Should the Congress heed Nader and pass a law to his specifications, of course, Nader's own "public interest" corporations would be taken over. For example, Nader has been one of those vociferously advocating an absolute prohibition on the use of DDT, which has saved hundreds of millions of lives and opened vast areas once unsafe for human habitation to the production of food. As a result of the campaign against DDT by Nader & Company, malaria, which had been virtually wiped out in the world, is wildly increasing in countries like India and Venezuela. According to the United Nations, in Ceylon alone the number of cases of this dreadful disease has risen from 110 cases a year before the Naderite campaign against DDT to more than two million cases at the last count.*

---

*The New Consumerists ascribe the extent of drug usage in the United States today —one in every three thousand Americans addicted—to the quality of life in this country and to the abuses of a profit-oriented society. They do not tell you that according to the *Encyclopedia Americana*, the ratio fifty years ago was one in

Despite the abounding evidence that Nader's panacea—the interference of government at every level—does more harm than good, and that more and more laws encourage more and more abuse, a poll taken some years back showed that a majority of all Americans felt that new legislation was needed to protect them from business. Two years later, in 1969, under the impact of Naderist propaganda, 68 percent called for consumer legislation. Nader's onslaughts on the government, particularly the Congress, have contributed to the drop in confidence in the national legislature to only 23 percent. Yet those who support Nader do not see any contradiction in his animadversions against the government and his insistence that an all-powerful government is the answer to all consumer problems.

The old-style consumerists used the marketplace to bring about improvements. If they determined that a product was faulty or overpriced, they laid their evidence before the consumer, hoping that he would not buy it. The attack was on the product, seldom on the producer. If the consumer was convinced by the consumerist argument, he stopped buying the product. The producer either went out of business or made improvements. It was a remarkably effective approach, developed by Consumers Research, since no housewife would buy a soap powder that did not clean, a toaster that did not toast, or a vacuum cleaner that left all the grit in a carpet.

Nader changed this by introducing the shotgun attack. Corporations were singled out not because they produced faulty merchandise—Nader had no fault to find with DuPont products—but because they were "paternalistic," because they allegedly polluted the atmosphere, because they did not hire enough women or blacks. He combined consumerism with environmentalism, but only when it suited his purposes. If unionized public workers endangered the health of New Yorkers by causing tremendous quantities of raw sewage to be dumped into New York harbor, to up their wages, Nader did not lash out at their "selfishness." He created a Project on Corporate Responsibility, but never spoke a word about the compulsory unionism which deprives workers of part of their earnings for the use of Big Labor activities which frequently run counter to the interests of the workers. He joined in the outcry for campaign spending "reform"—just so long as it

---

every five hundred Americans. A hundred years ago, one in every four hundred Americans was addicted to hard drugs.

was limited to the corporate community—but found no time to inform his public that admittedly illegal union spending greatly exceeds that of businessmen.

Nader's consumerism, in short, has little to do with the consumer, with improved products and services, or with the needs of the citizenry. It is an ideologically motivated effort to take control of industry from the producers and to turn it over to government and to the Naderites. This is statism, pure and simple—a kind of *national* socialism since Nader suffers from a suspicion of foreign countries bordering on xenophobia. It was this which converted and debased the legitimate concerns of the true consumers into a politically destructive force, which sowed distrust and suspicion of all the institutions of this country, and which led Paul Rand Dixon, who had labored in the consumerist vineyard as chairman of the Federal Trade Commission, to say of Ralph Nader:

"Im scared. What he wants is revolution."

14

Politics and Power

MUCKRAKER, CONSUMERIST, ENVIRONMENTALIST—THOSE ARE the descriptives that Ralph Nader applies to himself—at least publicly. Yet if there were such a word, the label most suited would be "powerist" in the manipulative sense. His obsession with the uses of power crops up through the very many interviews he has given to friendly reporters. The organizations he has created, the public acclaim that has come his way, even the hatred he has aroused—all of these he assesses in terms of the power he can wield, the leverage he can exert on the body politic. A man truly interested in the commonweal would care little about the source of the good works he constantly demands. But it was his interest in the mechanics of power which led him to urge the Congress to go into the courts to assert its ascendancy over the White House —a childish and grandiloquent suggestion demonstrating his total failure to understand the Constitution or the system of checks and balances on which it is predicated.

Though Nader claims to be above politics, his true claim to fame is as a political man, an operative of considerable dimension through murky sensibility. That he has always abused power is beside the point. So, too, is that side of him discerned by the columnist Marianne Means but thoroughly misunderstood by her when she wrote that "the personal characteristics that made Nader popular as a crusader are exactly the ones that would make him a disaster as a campaigner. He is inflexible; he would rather lose than compromise, which is not a good idea for a politician. He is abrasive and insulting; he once told a friendly congressman's wife he would never come to her home again if she served cocktails."

In any one else, this would be a disaster. But Nader is shrewd enough to know that insults are his stock in trade, that they enhance him in the public eye and contribute to the image he has sold the public that he is free and independent. If he ever runs for office, it will be as an *enfant terrible* who lets the chips fall where they may, who is afraid of no man. This is as necessary to him as his carefully cultivated pose of the poor immigrant boy with dirty nails who confounds his Ivy League opponents in their Brooks Brothers suits. It was the liberal *Washingtonian* magazine which far more astutely summed him up as a political pusher:

> Nader is an American Lenin too because he posits not a party elite but a self-conscious vanguard of citizenry, a professional army of do-gooders . . . Like all great revolutionaries . . . Nader is an incensed, driven man, deeply calculating and manipulative . . .

There are two other characteristics of the political operator in Nader which, paradoxically, do not contradict the *Washingtonian's* assessment. The first is his tendency to self-deception, noted by a former Raider, Anne Zill, who added that "much as I admire Nader and so much of what he is doing, when you begin by deceiving yourself you end up deceiving others." The second political attribute is the Leninist use of fear. Laurence Leamer, who wrote the *Washingtonian* story on Nader, was shocked to learn that those who spoke to him were terrified that anything they said that was critical would get them in trouble. Leamer reports that

> When I had finished my research I received a very emotional call from a former Nader associate late one evening. He said he had learned I was going to use his name in a context that might be considered critical of Nader.
> "I talked to a couple of Nader people today," he said. "And they say that I'll be in trouble if you print that story. It may be hard for me to get a job."
> "For God's sake," I said. "Do you realize what you're saying? Why are you so afraid? What kind of movement is this that makes people act this way?"
> "You're right," he said, "but please take the quote out."

Self-deception and terror are concomitants of political power, as Lenin well knew. So is a hard-headed pragmatism. Nader has always been aware that there are drawbacks to holding public office. He can run for office only if he is certain to be swept in. When the New Party, headed by Dr. Spock and Gore Vidal, grasped at Nader in 1972, hoping to make him its presidential candidate, Nader was aware that they were trying to ride on his back, rather than vice versa. The platform the New Party pieced together—which ran the gamut from an endorsement of homosexuality to a call for the abolition of CIA—was so outlandish that it could not but help to antagonize Nader. And the campaign song they wrote would have put off almost any candidate:

> There's nothing wrong with the land; it's the best.
> But I've taken it for granted like the rest.
> So as a good-intentioned resident
> Who up to now has been hesitant,
> I say its time we had the best man under the sun
> For President.
> Nader's the one!

The insanities and inanities of splinter-party politics were never what Nader had in mind. A serious bid from the left wing of the Democratic Party would have been something else. Nader has never really shut the door to that possibility, though he has said that "you don't have to be elected to be effective." This was true for him until, by a serious miscalculation growing out of a growing megalomania, he took on Congress and seriously tore his pants, turning many Democrats who supported him into antagonists or, much worse, amused observers. There is, however, no truth to Nader's contention that he does not endorse candidates. For reasons unknown, he tied himself to one of the least-respected members of the Senate, Vance Hartke. When Hartke ran for reelection, Nader gave him TV clip in which he said of the Senator from Indiana that he was the "most consistent and persistent voice on behalf of consumers in America." But no one asked why, sometime later, a Nader organization relegated Hartke to the ranks of senators with the "least integrity."

Politics, however, does not consist solely of running for office. It can also mean, as it has in Nader's case, the mobilization of money, time, talent, manipulation of the press, and so forth, for a political end. It was in this area that Nader showed his hand by trying to take over the drive for the impeachment of President Nixon. It was a typical Nader operation.

On the "Bloody Saturday" on which Special Prosecutor Archibald Cox was fired—and Attorney-General Elliot Richardson and Deputy Attorney-General William D. Ruckelshaus resigned rather than fire Cox—Cox's staff milled around the special prosecutor's offices in excitement and uncertainty. Cox's deputy, Henry Ruth, called an immediate staff meeting. Some sixty lawyers and other personnel trooped to the library only to find it crowded with newsmen who had been called to a press conference.

"What the hell is he doing here?" Ruth roared. The "he" was Ralph Nader. Anyone else would have been thrown out bodily for (1) having breached the tight security of the special prosecutor's offices and (2) calmly taken over part of the premises for his own purposes. In the presence of Nader's protecting angels, the press, little was said and no embarrassing questions were asked.*

Cox was fired and Richardson and Ruckelshaus resigned on October 20, 1973. Nader, who had been pushed off the front pages by the Watergate furor, saw an opportunity to make a comeback and add a new hit-and-run victim to his long list. The following day, the "nonpolitical" consumerist-environmentalist-muckraker attempted to muscle in on the publicity. A *Wall Street Journal* story in its October 22 issue proclaimed: "Nader to Help Lead Drive to Impeach the President":

> Consumer advocate Ralph Nader says he's going to help lead a "grass roots" drive to impeach President Nixon.
> Yesterday, Mr. Nader, who participated in an "impeachment vigil" outside former Special Prosecutor Archibald Cox's Washington office, accused Mr. Nixon of "practicing tyranny. He has overthrown the rule of law."
> Mr. Nader said he will work with groups such as Common Cause, a self-described citizens' lobby, and various labor unions in the impeachment drive . . .

Nader was simply adding the icing to what was already the political cake of the year—and realizing the fears of the Founding Fathers who wrote in *Federalist* 65 that "the most conspicuous

*Not a line of this appeared in the Washington papers. It took an enterprising publication, the liberal *New York* magazine, to tell the story several months later.

characters [in the prosecution of impeachable offenses] will . . . be too often the leaders or the tools of the most cunning or the most numerous faction, and on this account, can hardly be expected to possess the requisite neutrality towards those whose conduct may be the subject of scrutiny."

Certainly, Nader could make no claim of neutrality or objectivity. Over the years, he had spiced his speeches with invidious and antagonistic remarks about Richard Nixon and the Nixon administration. His first move, moreover, had no relation to the "grass-roots" drive he had promised. Joining with such extremist Democrats as Representatives Jerome R. Waldie of California and Bella Abzug of New York, Nader filed suit in Washington's Federal District Court to press for a judgment that the Cox firing was illegal. In a rather curious decision, Judge Gerhard A. Gesell ruled that the firing was indeed illegal but took no action, stating that he merely wanted to "declare a rule of law that will give guidance for future conduct." The declaration, however, did not seek to reinstate Cox or unseat his successor. The final order and declaratory judgment included what could only have brought chagrin to Nader. "At the injunction hearing," it stated, "the Court dismissed Mr. Nader as a plaintiff from the bench, it being abundantly clear that he had no legal right to pursue these claims"—something of a slap at the man who had joined the outcry for impeachment in the name of the "rule of law."

But Nader did not despair. Early in December 1973, he took part in an impeachment "conference" called by the Institute for Policy Studies, an organization which for years had been the strategy board and think tank for radicals, anarchists, and other extremists who trashed the national life in the sixties. Again Nader called for a "grass-roots" movement to topple the presidency and, with instant expertise, slashed at those on Capitol Hill who "prefer to wait until the White House disintegrates." Quick to offer a prediction, Nader added that "if the House [of Representatives] does not vote impeachment by March, there will be none." He even had harsh words about Cox: "When Harvard style meets White House perfidy, even when the law is on Harvard's side, the White House wins. Cox wanted to be above the battle." And Peter Rodino, the 64-year-old chairman of the House Judiciary Committee then beginning its deliberations on impeachment, Nader stormed, was "suffering a crisis of a lack of confidence" because, presumably, he had not immediately placed the hangman's noose around Nixon's neck.*

Nader won himself applause in some quarters for his entry into the impeachment lists. But he was also hurt. His consumerist-environmentalist following came from all parties and all walks of life. The hero of the battles over "pollution" and faulty appliances, however, had plunged into raw partisan politics—and to many, this shattered his image of the zealous crusader. And if congressional mail is any index of popular feeling, it was the "gut" issues of the economy which preoccupied the general public. In any case, even to those passionately wedded to the vivisection of President Nixon, Nader was something of a disappointment. The grass-roots movement he had promised to build never materialized simply because Nader did not have the time or the patience to follow through.

Though the restless Nader continued to denounce the White House and the presidency, he moved quickly on to other political causes. The public financing of both congressional and presidential elections, though too complex a question to lend itself to Nader's simplistic approach, briefly occupied his attention. Even some of Capitol Hill's strongest supporters of public financing of federal elections were admitting that there were problems, and opponents cried out that it would leave the field of political campaign spending to a Big Labor monopoly which could mobilize its legions—staff members on union payrolls—with impunity, thereby exerting ever greater control of the congressional process. Nader's fulminations against the "buying of elections" won him few friends among senators and congressmen who felt that his rhetoric was hurting the cause.

Nader's nonpolitical cloak slipped further in a speech during which he demanded that voting be made compulsory for all eligible Americans in order to "open up the electoral process." To many, this was arrogant and authoritarian. The constitutional

*There is more than a little irony to Nader's criticism of Rodino. Over the years, Rodino had been frequently charged with having Mafia connections. On February 1, 1966, Rodino met with Attorney-General Nicholas Katzenbach, demanding that the Justice Department suppress the publication of the *Valachi Papers*, a convict's exposé of the Mafia. When Katzenbach refused, Rodino threatened to take the matter up with the White House—behavior in marked contrast to his 1974 demands for an endlessly growing list of presidential tapes.

right to vote is coupled to the right not to vote. But Nader argued that 45 percent of those eligible to vote in 1972 had failed to exercise their right, and then plunged into open partisanship by adding that it was important that the "right people get into office." If the missing 45 percent had cast their ballots, Nader said, Senator George McGovern would have been elected—a statement as unsupported by evidence and as wide of the mark as much of his consumerist contentions.*

The friendly media, realizing what the impact would be of Nader's "plan" for making nonvoting a punishable offense, played it down. Representative Robert McClory of Illinois, however, could not resist comment. "The amateurish and highly inept effort of Ralph Nader in his report on the Congress has now been followed by [a] proposal that would punish free Americans who fail to register and vote. While Soviet-oriented societies with the one-party governments have embracred such a view, it is to be hoped that little support will be accorded Mr. Nader's latest fling in the area of 'participatory democracy.'" The *Chicago Tribune,* hardly a friend of the "ubiquitous Ralph Nader," quoted his statement that sending nonvoters to jail would be the "ultimate in democracy" and would deal a "decisive blow" to corrupt political machines. Lamenting voter apathy, the *Tribune* added:

> Far from viewing Mr. Nader's proposal as a "decisive blow" to machine politics, we think most machine politicians would welcome it. In Chicago's inner-city wards, for example, the biggest problem the political bosses have right now is in getting the faithful out to the polls. In many of these areas, it has been unfortunately axiomatic to say that the bigger the turnout the bigger the vote fraud . . .
> . . . If democracy is Mr. Nader's goal, he is approaching it by a curious route.

*A Census Bureau survey in 1973 disclosed that of those who had not voted in 1972, 43 percent just were not interested in the election, 8 percent disliked politics, 6 percent forgot, and 15 percent gave a variety of reasons. If Nader had his way, all of these people would be subject to fines or jail sentences. Another study during the same year, conducted by the National Assessment of Educational Progress, reported that only 44 percent of Americans between the ages of 26 and 35 knew how to use a ballot, and only 60 percent knew how presidential candidates were nominated. Of those who didn't know, 24 percent thought the nominees were selected by a national primary, with the rest believing that the nominees were picked by the House or the Senate, or otherwise profening ignorance of the process.

But Nader's essays into the political have not discouraged those who view him as presidential timber. Nicholas von Hoffman, a syndicated columnist and the *Washington Post's* extremist-in-residence, still beats the drums for Nader. In a November 30, 1973, column, he wrote:

> . . . Nader has probably saved more lives than Nixon-Kissinger have rubbed out. It is crazy. People say that America is too old and too crooked to take an honest president, but a Nader inauguration would be a gas. Can't you see him, after getting himself inaugurated, going over to the rooming house and packing his other suit in his beat-up bag, and then walking over to the White House and telling the guards at the gate that Nixon's fanfare blowers can go home because he's just signed the lease?

Nader was wiser than that. In his attempts at becoming a power in the political arena, he discovered that he was dealing with hard-bitten professionals, not corporation presidents who quaked in their boots when he looked in their direction. A twist of history, moreover, was casting doubt on his life-saving record—his claims to having "educated" Americans into understanding that "safe" cars made for safe driving. When the Arabs declared their embargo of oil and the Nixon Administration imposed a 50-mile-an-hour speed limit, highway accidents dropped dramatically, proving that it was the man behind the wheel—not the wheel itself—which caused fatalities. At the same time, enough people really interested in saving lives had come across conclusive Swedish studies which showed that it was not high octane gas or faulty automotive engineering which were the great killers of the road but what came out of a bottle purchased at your neighborhood liquor store.

But by this time, it was somewhat academic. In the first half of 1974, Ralph Nader was having a harder and harder time making the nation's front pages, and at least one poll showed that only 4 percent of the populace was taking its consumerist advice from the consumer advocate. He still had his adulators, but Nader was discovering that national scolds usually end up as national bores.

15

The Future of a Zealot

"WHAT AM I CONCERNED WITH?" RALPH NADER ASKED IN A rare moment of self-examination. ". . . The anal effusions of a society." A Freudian could not have summed him up more astutely. That is how he sees the country and its people. That is why he shows no pity or understanding for both his associates and his enemies. That explains his perpetual and monumental sense of outrage. All of society, to him, is an Augean stable which must be cleaned before he can allow himself to rest. Humanity is monstrous because it does not share his obsession. Everything about him is sullied by the *scatos* of existence. Alone of all men, he is clean.

The future for this zealot must therefore be a grey one. The law of diminishing returns, which applies both to economics and to human relations, has become operative. The young people who flocked to him by the hundreds as volunteers in his soap-and-water brigades still applaud when he mounts the lecture platform, but the word has begun to get around the colleges and universities that a stint with Nader is a traumatic experience. It is not the long hours and the slave wages that trouble those who were once ready to join his crusade. But they have heard the reports of the returned Raiders, and it is one which almost universally begins and ends with "I don't like him." He is far more concerned with the anal effusions of society than he is with people. The human equation is nonexistent for him.

One by one, those who joined him—shovel in hand, like minor-league Herculeses—have drifted away, some resignedly and some bitterly. A very few have remained—out of unshakable conviction in the "cause" or because the ego trip makes it worthwhile to accept the concomitants which go with the wearing of the Nader livery. But will they remain once the media which made Nader loses interest in him? He has been off the front pages for months, as his journalistic adherents have been caught up in the frenzy over Watergate and its "horrors." Or, to those for whom consumerism is a passion, there has been an increasing and sad awareness that Nader, like any other source, must be checked out. There has been too much static over charges that did not stand the test, of sensations that were not borne out by careful examination. For a while, he had Congress in his hand, but he lost it as a result of childishly unreasonable attacks on those who befriended him.

There was a time when the corporate community shuddered at the mention of his name or his slightest glance. There was consternation when his Project on Corporate Responsibility issued its ukase, summarized in a press release:

> The Project on Corporate Responsibility has written letters to the nation's 500 largest corporations demanding that they immediately establish procedures to ensure "continuing representation of the public interest" in the corporate decision-making process . . . [W]e believe that all corporations must undergo fundamental structural changes if they are to become truly responsive to society's needs. All corporations must realize that unless they change voluntarily, they will not escape the pressures that are building up for corporate reform.

The open threat sent board chairmen scurrying to the storm cellars, until questions began to be asked. If the corporate community was as scatological as Nader claimed, why did he limit himself to the five hundred corporations on *Fortune*'s list? Why not all corporations? What did responsiveness to society's needs mean— and who would gauge it? What moral authority did a tiny group of students, obviously ignorant of the world of business and industry, have to dictate to the nation? Were they equipped with anything more than an overweening intolerance and the comfort of their ignorance?

Most important of all, what could they do beyond calling names and shaking their fists? With Congress disenchanted and the media elsewhere detained, it became apparent that Nader's chain mail was, like the Emperor's new clothes, nonexistent. American industry would suffer for many years from the climate stimulated by Nader and his "reports"—but Nader had not created that climate. It had brought sweat and stinging eyes to the industrial community ever since the days of the New Deal when the tycoons turned tail and ran from epithets like "economic royalist." Nader had merely radicalized the vocabulary, steamed up the rhetoric, and lashed out more unrestrainedly. By the middle of 1974, there might be many in the corporate community who still sputtered at the irresponsibility of Nader's attack, but some were beginning to smile and a few to laugh.

It had become plain to growing numbers of so-called average citizens that, for all his preachments, Nader was not a serious man. Only Nader specialists could catalogue the many hundreds of objects of his disaffection and the victims of his hit-and-run attacks. But it did him no good when *Car and Driver*, echoing the sentiments of a sizable proportion of the citizenry, would say, "Nader's got a great record for indictments . . . but convictions have proved to be something else." Where he was once received with respect bordering on awe, a local publication now headed a story on his visit with "Scaring the Savages," and said of him:

> We in Boulder recently had the distinction of being visited by one of the nation's leading humorists. Ralph Nader devoted his talk to "the radioactive society," and like a witch doctor scaring ignorant savages with a transistor radio, he predicted that nuclear power was about to cause increased incidence of leukemia and cancer.
>
> What he did not realize was that in coming to Boulder, one mile above sea level, he exposed himself to a far higher level of natural radioactivity than in Washington, D. C., where the natural level, in turn, is about 2,000 times higher than that due to a nuclear plant. On his jet flights to Boulder and back, Ralph received nearly 100 times as much as he would get in 30 years living next to a nuclear plant . . .
>
> His funniest joke was this: "Check your home-owner's insurance. Why, if nuclear power is so safe, are the insurance companies unwilling to insure you for it?" In fact, they are not unwilling to insure you, they are just unwilling to pay twice for the same accident. Everyone in this country is insured against a nuclear accident by the Price-Anderson Act [by the private insurance companies and the government].

In the very early seventies, no publication would have treated Nader with such contempt. He had brought it on himself by speeches in which he said flatly that nuclear power was "finished"

151

because it was economically unfeasible, at a time when the utilities were clamoring for licenses and the scientists were approaching a breakthrough in designing a fusion reactor, the energy bonanza. And Nader was receiving this kind of treatment across the board. The true ecologists, who put human life above that of a few fish, were appalled by the epidemics which Nader's campaign against pesticides had brought on. Safety experts listened in shocked wonder to his smattering and yattering of ignorance on the subject. And so it was, down the line. In the past, moreover, where critics like Alice Widener had asked, "Will the Real Ralph Nader Stand Up?," the new refrain came from an old nursery rhyme, "Will he go East, will he go West / Will he go under the cuckoo's nest?" He had spread himself thinner than the mustard on a ball park frankfurter. Nader was everywhere, doing everything, accusing everybody. He became just too confusing for many people—a Keystone Kop run through the projector at double speed.

There are two other factors involved in Nader's decline. The first is that Americans have a short attention span. The man who has captured that attention must shout louder and louder, run faster and faster. If he is a breaker of icons, he must find new and bigger ones everyday to smash. The second is that prophets of doom, particularly those who upbraid men who are presumably about to die, who live on locusts and bile and demand that others follow their example, soon find themselves alone in the wilderness. In the history of his people, Flavius Josephus wrote of one Jeshua, son of Ananias, who in the Jersualem Temple suddenly began to shout:

"A voice from the East, a voice from the West, a voice from the four winds, a voice against Jerusalem and the Sanctuary, a voice against bridegrooms and brides, a voice against the whole people" ... All the time till the war broke out, he never approached another citizen ... but daily as if he had learned a prayer by heart, he recited his lament: "Woe to Jerusalem." Those ... who gave him food, he never thanked. His only response to anyone was that dismal foreboding. His voice was heard most of all at feasts. For seven years and five months he went ceaselessly, his voice as strong as ever and his vigor unabated, till during the siege ... [he] was going round the wall, uttering his piercing cry, "Woe again to the City, the people, and the Sanctuary!"—and as he added a last word, "Woe to me also!" a stone from an engine struck him, killing him instantly.

What has struck Nader is neither so violent nor so dramatic, but the hurt must be there. Public Citizen, Inc., the organization that was to give him a mass base and free him from the foundation handout and the favors of rich men, in its second year collected $983,000 instead of the $1.1 million it had collected in its first year. The difference was perhaps small—a cloud no bigger than a man's hand. But at a time when consumerism was still holding its own in the polls, a survey of five hundred American leaders who were asked what man they considered the "most influential" produced a surprise. In the midst of Watergate, 279 put Richard Nixon at the head of their list, only seven singled out Ralph Nader for that honor. The drop in contributions from the "little man" may have been the result of suspicion engendered by Nader's failure, despite prodding, to give an accounting of the millions he has collected over the past years. But the fall from influence, for the man who had humbled one of the most powerful corporations in the world, spelled out a grim warning. The hit-and-run driver, when he is discovered, has few friends in these United States.

Index

157

159

160